A Woman
Like Me

BLUE RIDER PRESS

a member of Penguin Group (USA) Inc.

New York

A Woman Like Me

BETTYE LaVETTE

with David Ritz

blue
rider
press

Published by the Penguin Group
Penguin Group (USA) Inc., 375 Hudson Street, New York, New York 10014, USA •
Penguin Group (Canada), 90 Eglinton Avenue East, Suite 700, Toronto, Ontario M4P 2Y3,
Canada (a division of Pearson Penguin Canada Inc.) • Penguin Books Ltd,
80 Strand, London WC2R 0RL, England • Penguin Ireland, 25 St Stephen's Green,
Dublin 2, Ireland (a division of Penguin Books Ltd) • Penguin Group (Australia),
250 Camberwell Road, Camberwell, Victoria 3124, Australia (a division of Pearson
Australia Group Pty Ltd) • Penguin Books India Pvt Ltd, 11 Community Centre,
Panchsheel Park, New Delhi–110 017, India • Penguin Group (NZ), 67 Apollo Drive,
Rosedale, North Shore 0632, New Zealand (a division of Pearson New Zealand Ltd) •
Penguin Books (South Africa) (Pty) Ltd, 24 Sturdee Avenue, Rosebank,
Johannesburg 2196, South Africa

Penguin Books Ltd, Registered Offices: 80 Strand, London WC2R 0RL, England

Grateful acknowledgment is made to reprint from the following:

"I Do Not Want What I Have Not Got," written by Sinéad O'Connor.
Copyright © EMI Blackwood Music (BMI).

"The More I Search (The More I Die)," written by Kim McLean. Copyright © 2012 Kim McLean Music (ASCAP).
Administered by Hippie Chick Twang Media, LLC.

"Before the Money Came (The Battle of Bettye LaVette)," written by Patterson Hood and Bettye LaVette. Copyright © Soul
Dump Music (BMI)/Bettye LaVette (BMI).

Library of Congress Cataloging-in-Publication Data
LaVette, Bettye, 1946–
A woman like me / Bettye LaVette with David Ritz.
p.   cm.
Includes index.
ISBN 978-0-399-15938-1
1. LaVette, Bettye, 1946–   2. Singers—United States—Biography.   I. Ritz, David.   II. Title.
ML420.L258A3   2012   2012026041
782.421644092—dc23
[B]

Printed in the United States of America
1   3   5   7   9   10   8   6   4   2

Book design by Michelle McMillian

This book is dedicated to
the memory of
Jim Lewis,
star maker.

A Woman
Like Me

A vicious pimp was precariously holding on to my right foot as he dangled me from the top of a twenty-story apartment building at Amsterdam and Seventy-eighth Street. It is as true as it is ironic that some months earlier this same man had met me at Small's Paradise in Harlem, where I was singing my semi-hit "Let Me Down Easy." The man had no such intentions; he was sadistic, callous, and impossibly gorgeous. He had wooed and won me by reciting long passages from the *Rubáiyát of Omar Khayyám*. He possessed the world's most mellifluous voice. When he took me to secluded Provençal bistros and ordered in flawless French, I practically melted into the brie. He dressed elegantly. He even sang beautifully. His charm was so prodigious that only he could break my obsession with Clarence Paul, Marvin Gaye's compatriot and Stevie Wonder's mentor at Motown. Clarence's marriage had not stopped me from pursuing him night and day. I lived for those few moments when Clarence and I could steal away to the dark end of the street. That's when I was seventeen.

Before I turned twenty, the debonair pimp had temporarily cured me of my misdirected passion for Mr. Paul. Mr. Wonderful wove a web of such subtle design that I mistook my prison for a palace. Little by little, he stripped me of all outside contacts. He showed me how his own women waited on him hand and foot, and he expected the same of me. He convinced me that it was my absolute obligation to bring him at least a hundred dollars a day. That meant turning tricks.

I am a woman who does not like admitting mediocrity at any task—particularly one where fucking is the centerpiece. Yet in all honesty, I cannot claim the status of a world-class whore. I tried but stumbled. It might have been that Mr. Wonderful warned me so vociferously about soliciting cops that when I started to work, every potential customer looked like a policeman. I did not prove a good earner. I had to rely on friends to give me the hundred dollars to avoid getting beaten by my man. Fortunately, I found one sweet john—Johnny Desmond, a singing star from the forties and fifties then appearing on Broadway with Barbra Streisand. He was a cultivated man, and we enjoyed stimulating intercourse, both intellectual and sexual. Johnny kept me in business for several months, and I remain grateful.

Finally, though, I saw the light. That light did not involve religion. My story is one in which Jesus will not be making an appearance. My feeling then and now is that if God is fond of black people, he has shown his affection only recently. What the hell took him so long? What the hell took me so long to see that I was aiding and abetting a raging asshole? Sure, Mr. Wonderful looked debonair in his pale blue Turnbull & Asser shirts and his shiny mohair suits, but at some point I had to look at myself and ask, *Why in the world am I putting up with this lowlife?*

On a balmy spring night I gathered up my nerve and said, "I'm gone."

"You stay," he retorted, "until I kick your ass out."

"I'm not asking," I snapped back. "I'm telling."

He responded by grabbing me by the neck, dragging me to the roof, and dangling me over the edge. The fact that the traffic down on Amsterdam Avenue was light was of no comfort.

"Bitch," he said. "There's only one way you're leaving. That's if I decide to drop you."

I knew the man was monstrous, but I did not see him as a murderer. Of course, I couldn't be sure, but I had to take that chance.

"If you think I'm worth the rest of your life in jail, then drop me."

"Fuck you," he said. "You'll never make it without me."

That's when he pulled me up, slapped me around, and told me to get out. I ran like the wind, leaving everything behind.

I hit the streets of Manhattan wearing a pair of shorts, a bra, and no shoes. I had no money.

Where was I supposed to go?

What was I supposed to do?

Drink

I was born into a heavy-drinking family. Early on I became—and remain—a serious drinker. I make no apologies for this. It's who I am.

I drank from conception; I drank in the womb because Mama drank every day of her life. She lived to be ninety-one and probably would have made it to a hundred if, because of her drunken state, she hadn't had a silly accident.

Daddy, who adored me, loved his liquor just as much. High blood pressure–induced strokes didn't stop him from drinking. A stroke killed him when he was forty-six.

My parents' grand enterprise, besides their children, was an at-home corn-liquor business where they sold booze and barbecue sandwiches. They filled the house with anyone looking for cheap drink and tasty food. A blues-blasting jukebox provided the entertainment. Among the happiest customers were the biggest gospel stars at the time—the Pilgrim Travelers, the Five Blind Boys of Mississippi, the Dixie Hummingbirds. The church entertainers didn't want to be seen in public bars, so my parents' home was the perfect spot. They loved to party and I loved hearing them sing.

They loved hearing me sing as well. Mama would set me in front of the jukebox and with "Let the Good Times Roll" blasting out of the speakers, everyone cheered as I pulled up my skirt and rolled my stomach in time with the music. By the age of two, I could grind to the groove.

Daddy was Frank James Haskins and Mama was Pearlina Johnson. They grew up in rural Louisiana. Before they met, Daddy had already been married. His first wife died in a fire along with their daughter, also named Betty. Mama had gone through two husbands, both younger than she was, and had a daughter, Mattie, my beloved sister and closest friend in life, thirteen years my senior. My mother was so gorgeous they called her Pretty Pearl.

Family legend said Mama spotted Daddy at the sawmill where he worked. As the planks rolled down the line, the men kicked them in a slick rhythm that flipped them over to be split with perfect precision. Supposedly Daddy was the best of the sawmill showmen. Mama liked his style and brought him lunch.

I guess lunch was good, 'cause before long they were keeping house. Mama had that New Orleans religion, the kind that let her go to Mass drunk every Sunday morning. In her version of Catholicism, God and hooch got along great.

Frank, Pearl, and Mattie migrated to the sandy beach town of Muskegon, Michigan, where I was born Betty Jo Haskins on

January 29, 1946. They set up their makeshift nightclub at home in the projects where we lived. There was no gambling or loose women, only a jukebox, booze, and Mama's homemade sandwiches. It was the perfect space for locals looking to relax.

Both my parents had steady day jobs. Mama worked for rich white women and picked up many of their social graces. Like many of the women of her background, she made class distinctions among blacks. She liked to say, "I'd rather be a goat than a nigger." Mama's cursing was restricted to the occasional use of "bitch," "bastard," and "hell." I never saw her naked until she was deathly ill. I'm not sure Daddy did either; I suspect that she demanded they have sex in the dark.

Mama cooked in the hallowed Louisiana tradition, making masterpieces with leftovers. Later in my life, guys who quit me came back just for Mama's cooking. For his part, Daddy demanded strict southern fare—pigs' ears, tails, and feet. I wanted French fries, but Mama said, "I ain't messin' up my potatoes by cutting them up into little pieces."

Mama sang to me. She'd sing blues by Clara and Bessie Smith, who had performed at the plantation where she'd lived. In her mind's eye, she carried images of those larger-than-life ladies. She also loved country and listened to the Grand Ole Opry on the radio. Daddy liked the cowboy singers Gene Autry and Roy Rogers.

Mama and Daddy fought long and hard, especially when I was young. Mama tells the story about how she was going to leave him after a big blowup. She packed up me and Sister, and bought seats on the Greyhound back to Louisiana. Being the loudmouth that I was—and am—I ran up and down the aisles telling my fellow passengers, "We're going to Mama's home because Daddy hit her and she called the police!" Later I learned the real story: It was Mama who had a history of hitting Daddy. When Daddy retaliated, she swore she was taking us with her and never returning. We stayed in Louisiana for about a half-hour before we turned around and headed back to Michigan.

As far as I was concerned, Daddy could do no wrong, which was also his attitude toward me. He was so protective that he wouldn't let me go to school in the rain. He was so devoted to Mattie that I was sure he was her biological dad. Not quite stocky but past skinny, Daddy had a face like the Indian on a nickel. There was a honey hue to his dark caramel coloring. He sported two hairstyles. The first was slicked back with Murray's grease. Then when a new process came along, he wore it fried, dyed, and laid to the side. His favorite fabric was gabardine. He loved gabardine slacks, but there was nothing he loved more than a drink. As much as he loved me, I once saw him take my roller skates to the pawn shop where he got them in the first place—all for liquor money. He drank too damn fast.

Daddy liked ladies and had no shame in taking me with him to meet his women. I had no idea that they were his special friends or that Daddy was having flings. I just knew that these ladies plied him with liquor. My guess is that my mother, fearless and headstrong as she was, had a couple of flings of her own.

My folks had no regard for money. They drank away whatever slim profits their corn liquor and pork sandwiches might have yielded.

Mama was more moderate in her drinking. Every time she hid the booze supply, Daddy tore up the house till he found it. If on a rare occasion he failed to find it, he ran out to one of his ladies.

Mama retaliated by getting in the car, turning on the ignition, and driving into a wall.

How did I weather this world of overwrought emotions?

No doubt, I was overwrought too, but I can't say that I was frightened. I knew that these two people loved me dearly. They protected me. They also provided an excitement that got into my blood. Music was exciting. Dancing was exciting. Partying was exciting. Seeing people grouped together in search of fun turned boredom to fascination.

I was fascinated by the interplay between Mama and Daddy. When I was very young the explosions were nonstop. The high drama between them was better than anything on TV. The break-up-to-make-up syndrome kept us on our toes.

After nearly two years in Muskegon, we moved to Pontiac, where we stayed for a minute before moving to Detroit. My folks had factory jobs at General Motors while Sister, who married at fourteen, stayed behind in Muskegon with her husband.

When I got to be ten, the drama subsided because of Daddy's strokes. His medical condition quieted the love storms, and Mama became his conscientious caretaker.

Sister was an angel, and her husband was a low-down dirty dog. He gave her nothing but grief. We all celebrated when Sister left him and joined us in Detroit. The problem, though, was that her next husband was worse. He was violent not only with Sister but with me and Mama as well. Sister was with this evil muthafucka—a degenerate gambler, cheater, and wife beater— for twenty years before someone did us the favor of murdering him. You could say that Sister had issues with men. And yet this same woman was the most wonderful human being I have ever encountered. She was the perfect daughter and sister. Her kindness knew no bounds. Her compassion was deep and true, her disposition upbeat and loving. She was one of the bright lights of my life.

Sister took me everywhere—to a Little Esther show, to the beauty parlor, to the department store downtown. I loved her company and her looks. She was darker than I was, and, given the prejudice of the times, that convinced her I was prettier. I wasn't. She was petite, with small arms, wrists, ankles, and legs. Her breasts were larger than mine, but my booty was bigger than hers. To an outside observer, we were almost twin images of each other.

I still remember Sister's admonitions.

Keep your brassiere straps clean.

Don't take money from one man and give it to another.

Wash your own panties.

Like Mama and Daddy, Sister liked to drink. She also loved to read, even though she read junk. She followed the soaps and, I believe, viewed life through the lens of those melodramatic stories. Looking back, Sister's life became one of those soap stories. And come to think of it, so did mine.

Three Steps

Some performers who start out young complain about their lost childhoods. Well, you're looking at someone who never wanted a childhood. I never wanted to do the things that kids were supposed to do. I related to the world of adults. I wanted to do what adults did. I wanted to drink and dance and smoke and, when I learned about sex, I wanted to do that too. I saw childhood as a silly preliminary to the real stuff, the fun stuff. I wanted out of childhood as soon as humanly possible.

I also wanted out of school the minute I got in. Mama sent me to St. Agnes Catholic School because she thought it was a good idea for me to mix in with white kids. I thought it was a good idea to take some of the corn liquor my folks were selling at home and sell small sips at school. Mother Ernesta, who took me on as her special project, didn't agree. She saw me as a bright girl in need of direction. All I needed, though, was a way to avoid Mother Ernesta.

Like all the teachers at school, the nuns were white. I was grown before I ever saw a black priest or nun. Mother Ernesta was also certain that, with discipline, I'd prove to be a top student. She saw that, although I read well, I didn't want to be bothered with details.

"Details are critical to true understanding," she said.

"Why?" I asked. "All I need to know about World War Two is that it was us against the Germans, the Italians, and the Japanese."

"But when did the war start and stop?"

"It started in the thirties. It stopped in the forties."

"But *when* in the forties?" she asked. "When was Pearl Harbor?"

"The day the Japs bombed the shit out of us."

"Why express it with vulgarity?"

"I'm guessing the guys who got their asses blown up saw it as pretty goddamn vulgar."

"Stop cursing! It does not become a lady. You must read your history book more carefully."

"I don't wanna read it at all."

"What *is* it that you want to do?"

"Smoke and drink."

"You say that to shock me, young lady. But I don't shock easily. I know you have a good mind and native talent. I've heard you sing."

"You have?"

"Yes, I've heard you sing in the schoolyard. Your voice is strong and clear. You have good diction. I'd encourage you to sing in the upcoming talent contest. Consult Sister Bradford, who leads the choir, and she'll find you suitable material."

Naturally, I didn't consult anyone. When it was time to perform at the talent show, I looked over the assembly of students, priests, and nuns, and gave them a taste of the Coasters' "I'm a Hog for You." The song talks about how one piggy went to London, another to Hong Kong, but me, I'm wigglin' over to your house to love you all night long.

As you can imagine, the kids started squealing in delight, but Mother Ernesta, poor lady, nearly had a heart attack.

She interrupted me halfway through, waving her hands as if the school had caught on fire. I was never asked to participate in another school activity.

If I had to be in school, I wanted to go to the public school where my friends were carrying on. Public school had places for lazy students like me to hide. But Mama, a wine-loving Catholic, saw religious school as a way to gain greater social mobility.

The mobility that interested me the most was the kind that would get me out of the house. By age fourteen, I thought I was ready to move out. This was the late fifties, when the music that spoke to me loudest was Etta James's "Dance with Me, Henry" and "Good Rockin' Daddy."

I was eager to find the right rockin' daddy. I don't know why, but my folks put me in a bedroom in our house with three steps under the window. It was as though those outside steps had been built to make it easy for me to climb out whenever I wanted—or for someone to climb in.

In 1958, a fourteen-year-old boy climbed in for the sole purpose of deflowering me. I was twelve. I didn't like him for his looks; I liked him because he was bad. He was manic and violent, and he was considered the biggest bully in our North End neighborhood. No one liked him, and the cops were always on his case. When he threatened to beat me up if I didn't give him sex, he didn't know that he didn't have to bother with the beating-up part. I wanted to have sex. I was curious.

Because I had no one to compare him to, I couldn't rank the bully's technique. He didn't last long and neither did the pain. I was relieved. I viewed my virginity as a burden finally lifted. The fact that my first lover—using that word lightly—was a notorious bad boy was an omen of things to come. He was a dangerous character who didn't survive long on the streets of Detroit. He came to a violent end.

My initial goal was simple: I wanted someone who could get me out of my house and into a mink coat. If sex was part of that, fine.

I met Alphonso Mathis, called Pinky, when I was thirteen. I went after him because he had a job at a dairy loading milk trucks, making $18.75 a week. He was also a slick dancer. The boy had Jackie Wilson moves. He could drift like the Drifters on "There Goes My Baby."

I also liked that his parents paid him no mind because he was one of eighteen kids. They were busy running after his siblings. That made him independent, and independence was my goal.

While I was working at getting Pinky, tragedy struck. My daddy, only forty-six, died of a stroke. I was devastated. Suddenly everything changed.

I need to get a little psychological here and say that once

Daddy was gone, I went hunting for him the rest of my life. He was everything to me. I had challenges with Mama—the older she got, the bigger the challenges became. Mama and I loved each other dearly, but the woman got on my nerves. Daddy never did. I adored him. As far as he was concerned, I could do no wrong. I never felt his judgment or his scorn. So his absence punched a gaping hole in my soul.

He left a little insurance money that let Mama buy a house on Trowbridge on the north end of Detroit. I still own that house. I still own the sweet love that Daddy offered me without condition or expectation. He saw me as someone special and never tired of telling me so.

Who was gonna tell me that now?

It was even more urgent now that I win over Pinky. He was cool. He was older. In the years to come, with one great exception, they'd all be older. Pinky also had enough quarters to feed the jukebox down at Mr. Jerry's, our teen hangout. We danced to Bo Diddley and Fats Domino. We'd watch *American Bandstand* on TV, and I learned to love Bobby Darin. I'd sit and listen to Bobby "Blue" Bland, who brought me to tears. I didn't know any other kids my age who were crying to Bobby "Blue" Bland.

I was proud to have won over Pinky. And at fourteen, when I learned I was pregnant, pride turned to happiness and happiness to fear. I was happy because I figured being pregnant meant Pinky would be mine and love me forever. I was scared because I knew Mama would kill me.

She tried. When I told her, she grabbed my hair, put her foot on my neck, and attempted to separate my head from the rest of my body. She flipped all the way out.

Pinky's reaction was panic.

"What the hell are we supposed to do?" he asked.

"You tell me," I said.

"I don't know. This hasn't ever happened to me before."

"It didn't happen to you, it happened to me. I'm the one having the baby."

"I'm gonna ask my mama what to do," he said.

"What's your mama gonna tell you? She already has eighteen kids of her own."

I was right. His mama didn't care, but his daddy did. His daddy said we had to get married. So, at fifteen, I married Pinky, the best dancer in the 'hood. In some sense it was mission accomplished—I found a way out of my house and out of school. Pinky and I got a little place of our own, right down the street from Mama and Sister, who promised to pitch in.

We ran over to Toledo, tied the knot before a justice of the peace, and, just like that, I was a happily married woman—at least for a minute.

The birth of Terrye was a beautiful thing. Everyone loved my infant daughter, saw her as a blessing, embraced her, and nurtured her with all their might. In short order, though, I saw that I was not cut out for motherhood. While Sister and Mama cared for Terrye, I decided I wanted to rejoin my friends. But I was not going back to St. Agnes and Mother Ernesta.

Northern High was different. Northern was where the cool gals and cute guys congregated. To get back into the swing of things, I decided to enroll at Northern. I'd never been to a public school but was certain I'd be happy there. I was confident I'd do better at my studies.

My confidence was misplaced. I didn't do better because of something I hadn't expected, something that was taking over my life. That something was, is, and will always be music. Ever since I was a two-year-old rolling my stomach to the backbeat, I had been drawn to music. What I was about to learn was the deepest truth of my life.

More than simply loving music, I *am* music.

Chapter by chapter, music is what drives my story forward.

Black Bottom

Seems like my marriage was over before it began—six months, seven months max. Pinky wasn't much of a husband and I wasn't much of a wife. I do admit, though, that the boy did give me something I hadn't had before—an orgasm. For that, I say, *Thank you, Pinky*.

When it happened, I thought I was having a stroke. Strokes were on my mind because of Daddy's death. The orgasm was so powerful that I was convinced I was dying. My heart beat like crazy as my limbs went limp. Because I was preoccupied with my health, I actually missed the pleasure part. It took me a while to realize that an orgasm was the goal of sex. By then, though, Pinky was long gone.

I left high school in the ninth grade when they told me I had to take swimming lessons. Northern had a fabulous pool, and everyone was expected to swim. Not me. I don't take to water.

It's even hard for me to take a shower when water's coming at my face.

"If you want to be excused from swimming class," said the principal, "your mother's going to have to come in and sign a form."

"I'm a mother," I said. "What do you need my mother for? Besides, she's working. She doesn't have time to fool with your forms."

"Then we don't have time to fool with you."

"You won't have to," I said. "I'm gone."

The only things I missed about school were those red-devil pills, the kind that got you high and hyper. So instead of going to Northern every morning, I'd go to the shack across from school and hang out with the pill poppers and weed smokers. That was our little teenage drug community, where no one was reprimanded or kicked out.

I heard some of the older kids talk about the Black Bottom, the entertainment area of colored Detroit centered on Hastings Street. They talked about the Flame, where big-time acts like Della Reese and B. B. King performed. They also talked about the slick operators and fast women who frequented the area. That talk fascinated me. So did the older guys who hung outside Northern High accosting the sexier girls. They were Black Bottom pimps looking to recruit. My first thought was *Choose me! Choose me!* but I didn't get chosen. Why not? I was shapely. I had a big booty and a cute face, but I guess that wasn't enough. Maybe I lacked that come-hither vibe that makes a successful hooker.

A girlfriend and I hitchhiked to Black Bottom so we could see it for ourselves. It was love at first sight. I loved seeing all those long Eldorados, all those fast-moving people, all the action on the street and in the clubs. If you had told me I could be a singer in one of those clubs, I woulda never gone home again.

Ladies of the night in stacked heels and push-up bras!

Pimps in green silk suits, fancy fedoras, and spit-polished alligator shoes!

This was life, this was Paradise Valley!

I just wanted to stretch out on the sidewalk and take it all in.

I just wanted to stay there forever.

I was never the same. *Never.*

A taste of Black Bottom had me searching for any place where there was music and action. A girlfriend told me about the Graystone Ballroom on Woodward Avenue where Berry Gordy, a part-time songwriter and full-time hustler, was signing acts for his fledgling local label called Motown. Mama warned me to stay away from the Graystone, which, of course, made it more enticing. She suggested that I stay home with Terrye, but she and Sister were doing a fine job of caring for my little one. Long as they were around, I knew Terrye was in safe hands. Mama liked to say to me, "Betty Jo, it's your red wagon. Either push or pull it." So I pushed it and went to the Graystone.

They were all there: Otis Williams and the Distants, who would soon become the Temptations. The great David Ruffin, who would soon lead the Temptations. The Miracles with green-eyed Smokey. Mary Wells, who was singing Smokey's songs.

In music-crazy Motor City, no one was crazier for music than I was. At an early age, I was listening to music that adults loved. I loved jazz. I loved Etta Jones's version of "Don't Go to Strangers." I thought that was the most sophisticated music I had ever heard in my life. Music gave me a crazy kind of confidence. I had a voice. I could project. I could belt it out. I was ready. But I had no entrée. I needed a connection.

I saw that connection in Johno, the first of many pimp-mentors who passed through my life. He was also from the West Side, where the pimps were classier and richer. At twenty-five, he was ten years older than I was. He was also possessive. I was his and his alone, not a working girl, but a girlfriend. Like Mama, Johno didn't want me around the Graystone.

"I don't want nobody looking at you, sweet-talking you, or even touching you," he said.

But given Johno's business obligations, he couldn't keep track of me all the time, so I snuck off to the Graystone on a regular basis.

By 1961, Motown was slowly starting to show signs of success. Even their younger singers, at eighteen or nineteen, were several years older than I was, but I had every intention of catching up. The Primettes, from the Brewster-Douglass projects, had become the Supremes, while the Marvels, from nearby Inkster, had become the Marvelettes.

The only place I went during that year was to my sick bed. After Terrye's birth, I had major medical problems. I was in the hospital when the girl in the next bed over was visited by her boyfriend. He had a handsome face, a black mohair suit, black patent-leather shoes, red socks, and slicked-down hair. When his girlfriend went to get her blood work done, he stayed in the room and introduced himself as Willie Jones, a singer with the Royal Jokers. I knew their hit on Atlantic, "You Tickle Me, Baby." Willie was deep Detroit. He talked about having been in a kids' choir with Jackie Wilson, Little Willie John, and Della Reese.

"I'm singing at the Parisian," he said. "You want me to take you down there when you get outta here?"

"I'd love that," I answered honestly.

A week later I was at the Parisian with Willie Jones. He had one of the most beautiful high voices I'd ever heard.

"I sing too," I told him that night.

"Cool," he said, "'cause I got a song just for a sweet little girl like you. 'Shut Your Mouth.'"

"I didn't say a word."

"I just said the name of the song—'Shut Your Mouth.'"

When he sang it to me, I kept my mouth shut.

"What do you think?" he asked.

"I love it. A song about a young girl who makes her mama mad by staying out late is perfect for me."

"Then it's yours."

Not much later, Willie was mine—or I was his. Any way you look at it, we became a couple. I'd found a way into the small world of Detroit's about-to-bust-wide-open music scene. In the early sixties, that scene was fluid. In the days before Motown turned into a tight unit—and ultimately an exclusive club—the hustling producers/pimps/promoters/music-makers all overlapped. There were no boundaries or rules. The game was a free-for-all. And I wanted in.

No one could keep me out of the Graystone. There, I made friends with Sherma LaVette, who called herself Ginger. She knew absolutely every singer and musician; she grabbed everyone worth grabbing. Ginger was the first real groupie I'd ever met, a superfan. I became a fan of hers and wanted to be with her every minute.

I had formed a girl group called the Diamonettes. We lasted for only a couple of weeks, and I don't believe Ginger ever heard us sing. But one night in the girls' room at the Graystone, I was doing "Bye Bye Baby" because the tile acoustics made me sound better than Mary Wells.

"Hell, girl," said Ginger. "You can really sing. You got something."

"You got something too," I said. "That LaVette name. I like it."

"Take it. It's yours."

At that moment Betty Haskins became Bettye LaVette. For years I fooled with the spelling, but essentially I've been Bettye LaVette ever since.

At the same time, Ginger said something else that changed my life.

"I got someone I want you to meet."

"Who's that?"

"Timmy Shaw."

"The one who sings 'Thunder in My Heart'?"

"That's him. He needs to hear you."

"He sure does."

Not only did Ginger know the singers and writers, she knew the deejays, promoters, and pimps. When I brought her home to meet the family, Mama hated her. I loved her to pieces.

When Ginger introduced me to Timmy Shaw, I saw a man who was extremely ugly. I had no desire for him, but I went to bed with him anyway. I realized that if I went with Timmy, I'd get to meet the entertainers. He was in the record business, he was talented, and that was enough for me.

"I think I should take you to meet the woman who's been making my records," said Timmy. "She's my writing partner."

"Let's go," I said.

We rode over to the West Side, an exciting move for me. Until then, I didn't know that part of town. The apartment was on Broad Street.

The woman, Johnnie Mae Matthews, looked like Humphrey Bogart after a bad fight. She had cuts up and down her face, and forearms as big as Popeye's. Ugly as sin, but she had a voice that could shatter glass. I knew her from her records. Her hit was "My Little Angel," a song my mother loved. Johnnie Mae sang in the powerhouse style of Big Mama Thornton with a smidgen of Ruth Brown thrown in for good measure.

So there I was, standing with two singers who had songs on the radio. This was the big time.

Timmy went to the piano and Johnnie Mae sang something written by her and Timmy, "My Man—He's a Lovin' Man." She sang the shit out of it.

"Now you do it," she demanded.

I started, but after a few notes, Johnnie Mae stopped me.

"Don't play with it, baby," she said. "Don't pamper it. Hit it. You can't keep it in. You got to sing *out*."

I started again, and again Johnnie Mae held up her hand.

"Look here, child, if I was a little younger and a lot prettier, I'd cut this goddamn song myself. But I'm giving it to you 'cause you got the right package to sell it. You young and fine. But if you gonna be shy singing these here words, ain't no one gonna buy nothing. When I'm talkin' 'bout 'My man, he's a lovin' man,' I might just as well be saying 'My man, he's a *fucking* man.' That's the feeling I want behind it. Now can you give me that fucking feeling?"

I could—and I did.

Now all we needed was another song for the flip side.

"Do you know Willie Jones?" I asked.

"'Course we know Willie," said Johnnie Mae. "Who don't know Willie?"

"Willie has this song, 'Shut Your Mouth,' that he said I could do."

"Willie got himself in trouble," said Timmy. "He's locked up."

"Don't worry nothing 'bout that," said Johnnie Mae. "If it's good, and if he said you can do it, I'll go to his jail cell and get his okay."

That's just what she did, and a week or so later, I was about to make my first record.

I couldn't have been more excited. Johnnie Mae and Timmy were hooked up with Robert West, who at that time had more juice than Berry Gordy. These were folks with several labels of their own and a history of hits. Johnnie Mae told West that she thought "My Man" was a hit.

They took me into a tiny studio and gave me great musicians. Johnnie Mae was there to make sure I gave it that funky feeling. I wasn't about to disappoint Johnnie Mae. My attitude was strong. I'm not saying I was Big Maybelle or Etta James or Tina Turner. But just as I knew my big booty demanded attention, I knew my big voice could do the same. Besides, I was high as a kite—not on smoke or wine, but on the idea of making a record. I was also amazed that it had happened so quickly. And even though I'd just turned sixteen, after recording "My Man," I instantly turned twenty-one.

Matthews and West said the song would come out on one of their labels—Northern, Reel, or Jam. I didn't care which one. I just wanted to see my name on a record and hear it on the radio.

It all happened, but in a bigger way than I could have ever imagined.

"That record's so hot," Johnnie Mae said to me, "that when Jerry Wexler heard it, *he* wanted to put it out."

"Who's Jerry Wexler?" I asked.

"One of the owners of Atlantic."

"The Atlantic record company?"

"No, the Atlantic Ocean. *Of course*, Atlantic Records."

"Atlantic Records is really putting it out?" I asked. "Atlantic, the one with the red and black label? Atlantic, who's got Ruth Brown and LaVern Baker and Ray Charles and Solomon Burke and the Coasters and Clyde McPhatter and the Drifters?"

"And now," said Johnnie Mae, "Miss Bettye LaVette."

For one of the few times in my life, I was speechless. Several seconds went by before I asked the only question that occurred to me, the only question that seemed to matter.

"Do I get any money now, Johnnie Mae?" I asked.

Johnnie Mae turned around instantly and slammed me against the wall. She grabbed my throat and said, "Bitch, you haven't even made any money. Just take that cute little ass of yours and go on tour."

I was scared to death.

Lover's Question

Back when I was eleven or twelve, Mama came home one day from Elma and Carl's record shop with a hot new song by Clyde McPhatter.

"Wait till you hear this, Betty," she said.

She put on "A Lover's Question." I loved it as much as my mother did. Daddy didn't feel the same way. He was in a bad mood. He'd been drinking—as had she—and wanted more. They were both drunk, but Daddy wanted to be drunker. Meanwhile, Mama had hidden his liquor. That was her only way of preserving it. They got into a screaming match. To make his point, he grabbed that 78 record, threw it on the floor, and smashed it to bits. Mama didn't protest; she simply ran back out to Elma and Carl's and bought another copy. When she defiantly put it on the turntable and cranked up the volume, Daddy repeated his record-smashing routine. Mama didn't lose a beat. She was out the door in a flash, and when she returned, she had a fresh copy of Clyde's masterpiece in hand. This time when Daddy destroyed it, Mama minded even less.

"I bought four extra copies," she whispered to me.

Daddy had to admit defeat. Clyde McPhatter was the winner. Before long, I was calling him my favorite singer. So you can imagine how I felt, four years later, standing in the wings of a fancy theater watching Clyde sing the thing live. I thought I'd faint.

Not only was I touring with Clyde McPhatter, but there was Ben E. King—the same King who, with "Spanish Harlem" and "Stand by Me," had two of the biggest hits in the country. Croaking Clarence "Frogman" Henry was also there, singing "You Always Hurt the One You Love," as was Barbara Lynn with "You'll Lose a Good Thing."

Atlantic put some muscle behind "My Man." It hit the R&B charts and quickly climbed past "Green Onions" by Booker T. and the MG's, the Contours' "Do You Love Me," and Esther Phillips's "Release Me." It wound up running neck and neck with the Four Seasons' "Big Girls Don't Cry." "My Man" dropped, by the way, the same week as Marvin Gaye's "Stubborn Kind of Fellow." Marvin had been insistent about singing standards exclusively in the style of Nat King Cole. But when that didn't produce hits, he saw his stubbornness as a problem—so he wrote a song about being stubborn and had a smash.

"You got a bona fide hit, Bettye," said Robert West.

I was literally going places. The tour continued, dropping and adding artists as we went along. On our night off in Montgomery, Alabama, West's hometown, we went to see the unknown Otis Redding. He was a big guy—broad shoulders and long, strong legs—as country as a barn and as sweet as sugar. We took a liking to each other and were booked on the same show at the Royal Peacock in Atlanta, the major black venue in Georgia.

Otis was from Macon. As a Detroiter, I saw myself, even at sixteen, as far more sophisticated than twenty-one-year-old Otis. After all, he wore shiny mohair suits and red socks. Tacky!

There was no question he could sing. "These Arms of Mine" proved that. He started flirting with me during rehearsals on a Friday. We moved along to after-the-show drinks on Saturday, and by Sunday we were on intimate terms. He saw me, he said, as "a cute little girl from Michigan," and I saw him as a sweet man with an easygoing way. Naturally, I was flattered that he was enamored of me. After a weekend of shows, he went his way and I went mine. When we met up again, our little fling was back on, but I never took it seriously. I never took him seriously when he said he wanted to marry me. He said Atlantic would love that because we were both on subsidiaries of their label.

"Aren't you already married?" I asked.

"No," he said. "My girlfriend back home is pregnant by me."

Whatever the case, I had no interest in being Mrs. Otis Redding. To me, he was simply a wonderful singing guy who shared my love for Roy Rogers and Dale Evans and country and western music.

During the tour, I also had a brief fling with Ben E. King. That was tricky because Ben had both a home wife and a road wife. That made me second to the second.

I also had my eye on Clyde McPhatter. I wanted to sleep with him, if only to surprise and delight Mama with the news. But that wasn't possible because he traveled with a high-class call girl from New York who kept him in diamond watches and gold cuff links. Man, did I want to be her! She was absolutely beautiful. Rightfully so, she saw me as a character out of *All About Eve*. That's why she never let Clyde out of her sight.

In January of 1963, I turned seventeen and found myself once again on the same bill as Otis. He and I were back at the Royal Peacock, where he opened for me. "My Man" was still red hot and his "These Arms of Mine" had just begun to take off. His show was much more elaborate than mine. He had his own band. I basically had one song and a few pickup musicians. But that song was still getting me over and, even better, Atlantic was talking about me cutting another one. First, though, I traveled to Miami for a show at the Knight Beat in the Sir John Hotel.

The poster outside the club gave me top billing. Coming attractions included Redd Foxx, Jerry Butler, Maxine Brown, and Chuck Jackson. It was my first trip to Florida, and I was about to make a splash—except for one thing. I lost my voice.

"Ladies and gentlemen," said the emcee. "It's star time. Here she is, all the way from Detroit, Michigan, the little lady with the big voice. Please give a big Miami welcome to Miss Bettye LaVette."

I got up there, looking all cute, feeling all perky, but when I opened my mouth, all that came out was a croak. I was hoarse as hell. In those days, I never stopped talking. I was so excited to be on the road, I never wanted to go to bed for fear of missing something. I had to meet everyone and be in every conversation. As a result, my voice was gone.

It wasn't God who intervened on my behalf, but the next best thing—Little Willie John, among the greatest of all singers. A fellow Detroiter, he felt my pain. He jumped onstage, put his arm around me, and broke into his big hit, "Talk to Me, Talk to Me."

By the time he had warmed up the audience, my voice was back and I made it through. Grateful to Willie for saving my young ass, I took my bow, went to the dressing room, smoked a joint, and headed back to the club where a table had been reserved for me. I needed a drink. When I sat down in a chair facing the stage, though, some man said, "You can't sit there."

"Why not?"

"That's Marrie Early's seat."

"Who's Marrie Early?"

"You don't know Marrie Early?"

"I wouldn't have asked if I did."

"Everyone knows Marrie Early."

"Everyone except me," I said, sitting where I wanted to sit.

"That's Marrie's seat," the guy repeated. "That's where she sits every night."

"Every night but this night," I said.

"I told you once," said the man, "and I'll tell you again. That there seat is reserved for Marrie Early."

Something in his face told me not to fuck with him. So I left the chair empty and took another one.

For the next hour or so, all the talk at the table was "Where's Marrie?" "Wonder when Marrie's getting here?" "Sure hope Marrie gets here soon."

I thought to myself, *This Marrie Early must really be something.* She was.

Marrie Early's late entry to the Knight Beat was one of the great moments of my life. The minute she walked in that place, every head turned. If I thought I was the star that night, I couldn't have been more wrong. Marrie Early stole the show.

She walked in wearing a clingy white linen suit with nothing underneath. She had flawless caramel-colored skin, alluring eyes, double-rolled eyelashes, and a smile that lit up the night. She was beyond beautiful. She was small in stature—my size—but with bigger breasts, a smaller waistline, and wider hips. I later learned she had posed for a centerfold in *Jet*. You'd expect a woman this drop-dead gorgeous to be haughty. Not Marrie. She was a sweetheart.

"Baby," she said to me, "can't tell you how much I love that song of yours they're playing on the radio. Everyone down here's been talking about it." She spoke softly in a southern accent with a tone reminiscent of Marilyn Monroe.

"Really?" I asked.

"Yes, sugar, everyone. You know Sam Moore and Dave Prater?"

"I don't."

"They call themselves Sam and Dave. Out-of-sight singers. They're my best friends. They've been telling me you're the best singer they heard since Ike found Tina."

For being one of the world's best-looking women, Marrie was not interested in talking about herself. She talked about you. She made you feel good about what you were doing. She became one of my closest friends in life and, in many ways, a model for my sexual behavior. When it came to sex, Marrie was as free as a bird. If she liked you, she fucked you.

I'd guess you could have called Marrie a prostitute except for this fact—the men who gave her money for love did it without being asked. Guys *threw* money at her. I can't tell you the number of men—even devoted lovers of mine—who would testify, "Never had no pussy like that. Never had and never will."

I adored Marrie. So did every man in show business. She had suitors everywhere. The girl was international. She had guys who took her on cruises, guys who sent her jewelry, guys who paid her house mortgage. And the funny thing is that they were okay with Marrie having other guys—as long as she had them. No matter how rich or famous a man might be, he knew he could never own Marrie Early. She belonged to mankind.

Marrie was queen of Miami, a city that didn't even like blacks. But there was no man—black, white, or orange—who didn't like Marrie. Of her many wonderful qualities, the best was her freedom. She was free to fuck whomever she wanted, and her lover was free to do the same. If Marrie was out with a man who suddenly saw another chick who grabbed his attention, she'd say, "Go on, honey. Don't bother me none. I'll find my way home."

Marrie's home was supercool. She was the first single woman I'd met with her own house. That's where I learned that you could have lobster at home. It was also where I saw my first walk-in closet. And talk about clothes! Marrie designed and sewed her own. She had a real feel for showbiz outfits, and over the years she made me dozens of gowns.

"If you could sing or dance, Marrie," I told her, "I'd have to kill you. You're too talented as it is."

She laughed away compliments and turned them back on you. "You're the artist," she said. "I just sew."

Marrie had a relaxed attitude about everything. She surfed the wild waves of life with extreme poise and grace.

One time I was in her living room when she was back in the bedroom with a man. The doorbell rang. I went to see who was there. It was another man. He said he had a dinner date with Marrie. I went to the bedroom to tell Marrie what was happening.

"Shit," she said, "I'm too tired to get out of the bed and get dressed. Just have him come back here and join us."

He did what he was told, happy to have Marrie on whatever terms pleased her.

It wasn't purely sex that drove Marrie to men. It was more her desire to please them. She had a heart for people. She got great satisfaction in pleasing everyone. She used sex, but in a fascinating way.

Take Marrie's cousin. Because of her fluctuating financial circumstances, at this particular time Marrie was living in his house. He didn't like all her men coming around and threatened to kick her out. Marrie concluded that her cousin was confused about his own sexuality. She thought he had eyes for her men. But she also thought he needed to experience some serious sex with a woman. That's why she said to me, "I think we should both fuck him. I think having us both at once might clear his head."

That's what we did and, sure enough, Marrie was right. Cousin felt great afterward and left her alone to live in his house.

If I called Marrie in the middle of the night from Chicago to tell her I needed a thousand dollars to get out of jail, she'd get me the money in a minute. So naturally, I'd do anything for her, including helping her fuck her cousin blind.

I remember that when Marvin Gaye met Marrie, he turned to me and said, "Bettye, if you had legs like that, I'd love you all night." I'm not sure Marvin loved anyone all night long, but he did love big-legged women. Like nearly all the women who knew him, I'd been chasing Marvin and getting nowhere. Riding high with "Stubborn Kind of Fellow," Marvin also hit with

"Hitch Hike" around the same time Jerry Wexler called from Atlantic to say that he wanted another single from me. By then Robert West had become my manager.

I saw West as a cool old man with the right connections. He managed the Fabulous Playboys, a group he renamed the Falcons. They had a huge hit in the late fifties, "You're So Fine," and, at one time or another, their members included Eddie Floyd, Joe Stubbs, Mack Rice (who wrote "Mustang Sally" and "Respect Yourself"), and Wilson Pickett. Like me, the Falcons recorded for Atlantic, as would Pickett later on.

When West took me to United Sound to record my second single, "You'll Never Change," we used the Playboys who were replacing the original Falcons.

By then, I was living with one of the Playboys, Alton Hollowell, whom we called Bart. On that same session, Don Davis, a major Detroit character who later produced Johnnie Taylor, played guitar. (I never liked Don or saw his talent. When I needed help, he was conspicuously absent.) We were all convinced that "You'll Never Change" would be a bigger hit than "My Man— He's a Lovin' Man." We were all wrong.

My work life meant a lot of time away from my daughter. Some people said I was wrong to leave Terrye with Mama and Sister. But to those people I'd like to quote the song that says, "If I should take a notion to jump into the ocean, ain't nobody's business if I do." I felt my business was singing. Fortunately, Mama and Sister felt the same. They realized motherhood was not my thing. Show business was. My family never let me down. In essence, Terrye had three mothers—a doting grandmother, a loving aunt, and, in third place, an often absent mama doing all she could to pay the bills.

Was I guilty then? Am I guilty now?

I wouldn't be human if I didn't live with some degree of guilt. When it comes to my daughter, love and guilt go hand in hand. But did guilt overwhelm my need to get out there and do what I knew I was born to do?

Hell, no.

Bacon Fat

Many men have already run in and out of my story. And there are many more to come. Some are barely remembered; others are badly remembered. I recall many with gratitude and love. It's a mixed bag. But there are a few who demand a chapter of their own. The first of those is Clarence Paul.

I loved Clarence, adored Clarence, worshipped, pursued, and pushed my relationship with Clarence to the absolute limit. I did everything in my power to make Clarence Paul my man and, at the end of the day, he never was. I was merely one of his ladies. He thought I was cute. He liked the way I sang. I made him smile and laugh. He appreciated my fire. But I was the sideshow, never the main attraction. For more years than I'd like to recall, that was good enough for me. When it came to spending time with Clarence, I'd take anything I could get.

Who was Clarence Paul?

A cold-blooded music historian might identify him only as Stevie Wonder's first caretaker and producer at Motown. He molded Stevie's early music and, as Stevie would later tell the world, "He became the father I never had." A kinder and more serious scholar would see him as an enormously talented musical mind. His real name was Clarence Pauling. He was born in North Carolina where he and his brothers formed a gospel group, the Royal Sons, who became the "5" Royales after turning secular. They hit with "Baby, Don't Do It" in the fifties, but couldn't sustain a career. Clarence came to Detroit where he met Mickey Stevenson. They had a singing duo that didn't find much success, but when Mickey went to Motown as an A&R man, he brought Clarence along for the ride. It was Clarence and Mickey who, along with Marvin, wrote "Hitch Hike."

The Motown company line is that it was one big happy family. Bullshit. Motown was a bunch of tight cliques. Everyone was looking to position himself in the right clique. Marvin, for example, who came to Detroit from D.C. when Harvey Fuqua started working at Motown, got in good with the Gordy family. Harvey hooked up with Berry's sister Gwen while Berry's sister Anna grabbed hold of Marvin, who was seventeen years her junior. Marvin had been one of Fuqua's Moonglows, the doo-wop group that had hit with "Sincerely" and "Ten Commandments of Love" back in the fifties. Like Clarence, Harvey saw that doo-wop was dying and came to Detroit where producer-pimps were making money.

When I fell into the Detroit music scene, I didn't know any men who weren't making money off women. Whether the women were actually whores or ladies singing soul songs in the studio made little difference. Men were running women. This is the situation I accepted, even embraced. This was the reality I worked with. I liked many of these pimp-producers. I liked the edgy life they led. They were exciting, unpredictable, and sharp in mind and dress. When they had money, they let you know it by the cars they drove and the clothes they wore. When they didn't have money, they found a way to keep steppin' and stylin' all the same. They were survivors who taught me to survive. I don't mean that there weren't serious assholes among them, but every culture has its assholes. In this culture, they were my men and I was their woman.

Out of this culture came Clarence Paul, talented, charming, drop-dead handsome, and married. The first time I saw him, I was gone. It happened like this:

I was at a club in Detroit called Lee's Sensation. Nat Lee was the proprietor.

I'd describe Lee as one of my "investors." As my story unfolds, you'll see that for the next four decades that group includes club owners, numbers men, pimps, politicians, and Baptist ministers. These were gentlemen who supported me in a variety of ways. In Lee's case, he gave me not only a platform where I could be Bettye LaVette, but free drinks along with endless encouragement. I'm forever grateful to my "investors."

Andre Williams was another supporter, an early Motown producer and former doo-wopper looking to be born again in the world of sixties soul. He came out of the Five Dollars and, on his own, had a hit called "Bacon Fat." Like most of the men who befriended me, Andre was ten years my senior. We became instant buddies and remain so to this day. I was watching Andre perform at Lee's Sensation when Clarence Paul walked through the door and looked right at me—right *through* me. Everything about him was beautiful.

"Bettyelavette?" he asked, slamming my names together.

"Yes," I said.

"Come here," he ordered.

I did. And I never came back.

I left with Clarence that night. He put me in a shiny new Eldorado that later I learned was Andre's. At the time, I thought it belonged to Clarence. I thought the world belonged to Clarence. We rode off into the night and I was his.

In an era when most black men were reluctant to please women with oral sex, Clarence had no such reservations. Maybe that's why he had more women than anyone. By word and deed, he let the ladies know that his business was pleasure.

That night I took him home to the basement bedroom I occupied in our house on Trowbridge. I had painted the room a cool blue and furnished it tastefully. It was my private den. It had its own separate entrance. It allowed me to conduct my romantic life without involving the rest of the family. My daughter never met the men with whom I became involved. She never saw me in bed with anyone but my husbands.

Before my male friends left, I encouraged them to leave a message on the wall. It became a tradition. I was surrounded by love notes and good wishes, happy memories of happy encounters. Of all of them, none was more satisfying than my time with Clarence.

The way Marrie Early deeply loved men, Clarence deeply loved women. Of course, sex was a major ingredient, but it was more than that. Unlike a lot of guys who ran off at the mouth, Clarence was a man of few words. He had a calm and quiet aura.

When you were with Clarence, he gave you his all. He looked at you, listened to you, felt you. He loved your company and you loved his. He had warmth I couldn't resist. Out of all of his many extramarital affairs, I'm proud to say that ours lasted the longest. It took me damn near forever to get over him.

This night of nights, when "Bacon Fat" drew me to Clarence, happened in 1963, the same year as Stevie's first number-one hit, "Fingertips," written by Clarence and Hank Cosby. Stevie was thirteen, I was seventeen, and Clarence was thirty-five. Marvin had another hit with "Pride and Joy" while my second single for Atlantic was sinking fast.

In these early days of Motown, I had attitude. I saw myself as a cut above the local label. The Supremes and Temptations still hadn't broken through, although Mary Wells, the Miracles, and the Marvelettes were doing well. My friend Martha Reeves and her Vandellas were climbing the charts with "Come and Get These Memories" and "Heat Wave." But my head was high because I was an Atlantic artist, the greatest R&B label of all time, where Ray Charles became a superstar and Solomon Burke and the Drifters were my labelmates.

At the same time, I wasn't too proud to walk over to the Motown bungalow on West Grand Boulevard and sit around all day in the hopes that Clarence would emerge from the studio and spend time with me. Sometimes he did, sometimes he didn't. When he did, the sun came out and the world was right; when he didn't, I was disappointed but not defeated. Much as I adored Clarence, I knew he wasn't about to leave his wife. Meanwhile, there were other guys who wanted to be with me, other men more than willing to help me get on with my career.

Even though this is Clarence's chapter—and certainly Clarence was the object of my most intense romantic concentration—there's another man who, like Clarence, became a friend, mentor, and sometime lover. He was a Detroit pimp named Ted White.

I call Ted a pimp because he freely called himself a pimp in my presence. He proudly described himself as such. Everyone who knew him well saw him not only as a pimp, but as one of the city's most prestigious operators in that highly competitive field. I know that since those days Ted has turned himself around and become a model citizen. I applaud his makeover. But to tell the truth—which is the whole point of this book—I liked him back in the day when he was not walking the straight and narrow. I thought Ted White was one of the coolest guys I'd ever met.

I met him in 1963. I was playing the Palladium Club, which had just opened. Ted came in to book his wife, Aretha Franklin, who would follow me with a ten-day engagement. Ted caught the end of my show and then introduced himself. He wanted to know if I was Jimmy Joy's woman. I said no. Jimmy Joy was the biggest pimp in the city—the man Ted aspired to be. He wanted to know if I was attached to anyone. I wasn't. Did I want a drink? I did.

I found Ted intriguing. I had no strong sexual desire for him, but I saw that he wanted me. I also saw that he was extremely well groomed. He wore black slacks and an expensive black silk jacket. There was nothing gaudy about his dress. His jewelry was tasteful, a vintage Rolex watch, a set of discreet gold cuff links. He was cultivated. He was a reader. You never saw Ted without a history or psychology book. Rarely did you hear him curse. I later learned that he was admired and envied by his colleagues for his ability to attract women. What he had in abundance—and what they lacked—was class. It helped that he was handsome, but it was his aura of intelligence and cool composure that made the ladies want to turn tricks for him.

Of Ted's many fine qualities, the best was his teaching ability; he knew how to instruct a woman on the art of being a lady. He knew where to take her to buy elegant clothes; he could distinguish one expensive French perfume from another. It was Ted who taught many of us the nuances of stylish dress. In those days, we young girl performers tended to be loud and brash, onstage and off. Ted was the first to say to me, "Look, baby, when you're out in public, in a restaurant or at a club, modulate your voice. Don't squawk. Speak. A whisper gets more attention than a shout. Men like women who talk softly."

"I can't do that," I said. "I get too excited."

"Then control your excitement."

"I can't control shit," I said.

Ted laughed. I could tell he liked me. It was more than the fact that I was seventeen and Aretha was twenty-one. He liked my free spirit. That spirit led to his bed. Over the next several days, we started what would be a dalliance that, with long respites, lasted decades. He became a good friend and a much-needed mentor. When I got into trouble and needed money, Ted was always there to help. Of course, I wasn't his only other woman. He had many ladies stashed in apartments throughout the city. Between his prostitutes and girlfriends, the man led a busy life. Yet he negotiated those many relationships with skill and style.

When it comes to the history of Aretha, Ted has been unfairly maligned. I think he helped her enormously. He told me how Aretha's famous preacher father disapproved of their marriage. That motivated Ted even more to make sure that Aretha found fortune and fame. His main earner was a gorgeous prostitute men found irresistible. I adored her. And I emulated her. And I always aspired to be the "lady" she appeared to be. Ted further explained to me that it was important for him to be a manager and that you had to live up to his standards in order for him to work with you. He and Aretha also later managed Walter Jackson, whose first recording, "I Don't Want to Suffer," was released the same week as *my* first recording. We did what were then called "record hops" together.

Ted was a great friend of Dinah Washington's—as was Aretha's dad. Ted used to say that his dream was to have Aretha kick Dinah's ass—figuratively, of course. Dinah was the reigning queen, and if Ted could tutor the new queen, if he could rigorously train and prepare Aretha for the crown and actually pull off her coronation, he'd accomplish a lifelong dream. Well, that's just what he did.

A word about physical violence. I realize it's politically incorrect to admit this, but the sight of a man slapping a woman did not horrify me. Context is everything. In the context of the Detroit showbiz culture of the sixties, men slapped their women around. They just did. It may sound radical to say so, but some women needed that. Some women even benefited from that. We all knew—we saw it with our own eyes—that Ted was slapping Aretha around. But without Ted's grooming, Aretha would never have been a superstar.

Same with Ike and Tina. I hated how Hollywood pictured Ike as a sadistic ogre. There was much more to the man than the movie revealed. Without Ike, there would be no Tina. He created her, reshaping her to become another person. Offstage he called her Ann. Onstage she was Tina. Through her long years with Ike, hundreds of men wanted Tina. Hundreds of men would have whisked her off in a hot minute. Tina could have left Ike at will. She chose to stay because she wanted to learn the lessons he had to teach. And those lessons resulted in her becoming a million-aire many times over.

As you can see, I'm a man's woman. It's fascinating—and easy—for me to see life from a man's point of view. Maybe a psychologist would say I identified more with my dad than my mom. Maybe that same psychologist would say that because I lost my dad early, I kept searching for him in all these older guys. But I didn't go to a psychologist. Psychology is an intriguing thing. God bless all the psychologists, but therapy was not part of my life, then or now. I acted out of instinct. My instinct was to survive as a singer and prevail as a person. It didn't take a genius to realize that men held the key to that survival. Aside from a notable excep-tion like Johnnie Mae Matthews, men had a stranglehold on the industry that interested me most. Women were their props. The only question was what kind of prop was I going to be.

The Apple

Nineteen sixty-three and sixty-four were big years. The Four Tops had their first Motown hit, while the Temptations and the Supremes finally broke through. Berry Gordy was riding high. It didn't look like anything could bring him down until he got the news that shook him to his core: Mary Wells, his first superstar, was leaving. Mary had turned twenty-one and her lawyer argued that the contracts she had signed as a minor were invalid. It was her manager and former husband, Herman Griffin, who was moving her from Motown to 20th Century Fox Records. All this had a huge impact on me because Griffin was in business with Robert West, my manager. The Griffin–West combination, with Mary Wells in their camp, was a sure winner. They were already planning a tour and promising me lots of big gigs.

After my second single flopped, I needed encouragement. By then, Bart Hollowell and I were living together on Trowbridge.

He was a good man who babysat Terrye and ran errands for Mama. Bart would do anything for me. Meanwhile, I was still messing around with Ted White and wildly in love with Clarence Paul.

I ignored Sister's advice not to take money from one man to give to another. I took money from Ted and gave it to Bart to help us with our living expenses. I didn't see any other way to get by.

Professionally, my stock had fallen. I was down to playing local gigs. I was opening for Johnny Nash at Phelps Lounge. I didn't complain, because the backup band, later known as the Funk Brothers, was one of the best anywhere. They were the guys who played on dozens of Motown hits and were then led by pianist Earl Van Dyke. Jack Ashford was on vibes, James Jamerson on bass, and Benny Benjamin on drums. The problem wasn't with the music but with the money. I was paid next to nothing and barely getting by.

My mind kept asking the same questions: *If I'm an Atlantic artist with a solid hit to my credit, why am I starving? Why isn't Atlantic doing more for me?* My friends were asking the same questions. They had the same doubts. Had my label in New York forgotten about me? Did they care?

When Robert West went to New York to hook up with Herman Griffin, I thought that problem would be solved. Mr. West would meet with Jerry Wexler to see whether Atlantic was serious figure about promoting me. If not, Mr. West would find another major label for me, just as Herman had found 20th Century Fox for Mary. Mr. West was also putting together a tour. All my hopes were on him.

Katherine West, Robert's wife, was making dresses for me to

wear on that tour. I was at her house for a fitting when the call came: her husband, Robert, had been shot.

The story was that Robert and Herman Griffin had been drinking and began arguing over contracts. Robert blew a fuse and went for his gun. Before he could fire it, Herman pushed Robert's hand so that Robert wound up shooting himself in the eye. Robert wasn't dead, but he'd never be the same.

I couldn't believe it. My manager—my hope for the future and the man about to send me out on a major tour—had tried to shoot Mary Wells's husband, only to wind up shooting himself.

How to react? What to do?

All I knew was this—I had to get out of Dodge. Detroit wasn't working for me. These little ol' club gigs weren't paying. Without a manager to look after my career, I had to look after it myself. If I wanted the big time, I'd have to get to the big time. I had to get to New York. I had to pack my things and put my ass on a plane.

The truth is that for as long as I'd been seeing photos of glamorous stars in glamorous nightclubs in *Jet*, I'd been looking for an excuse to go to New York. I'd do anything to get there. It's taken me a lifetime to realize the foolishness of that move. These days I tell young people in show business: Don't go to New York or L.A. unless you're asked. In 1964, no one had asked me to go; no one wanted me to go. But, me being me, I went anyway.

Sister and Mama—bless their hearts—supported me in all my decisions. After all, I'd made more money than any of them. I was the first in my family to make a hundred dollars in a single day. They saw no reason why I couldn't be an artist as big as Mary Wells. If that meant going to New York, so be it. They'd care for Terrye.

Bart wasn't happy about my leaving him, but Bart, for all his sweetness, didn't carry much influence. Clarence Paul and Ted White gave me enough money for a plane ticket and a few weeks' worth of expenses.

The night before I left, I was at Phelps Lounge where I met a man who would change my life.

"Miss Bettye LaVette," he said, "you're a good singer but you need training."

"Who the hell are you?"

"Jim Lewis."

"And who gave you the authority to tell me what I need?"

"I'm an exec at the musician's union. Been around music my whole life. Played trombone for Jimmie Lunceford. I know singing, and especially female singing. You need training."

I looked up at this guy. He was over six feet tall and spoke with a deep voice. He was in his early forties. I was eighteen.

"Look, mister," I said to him. "You're saying I need training. Well, I'm saying I need to get to New York."

"When are you going to do that?"

"Tomorrow."

"Fine. But take my card and call me when you get back."

"I ain't coming back," I said. "I intend to make it in New York."

When I arrived in New York, my first reaction was to die in the middle of Broadway. Just lie down and let the cars and yellow cabs roll over me. That's how happy I was. I could have ended my life in the middle of Manhattan and felt like, having seen this magic land at least once, I had lived. I fell for the city almost as hard as I'd fallen for Clarence Paul. The energy got me. The energy pushed me forward. The first thing I did was run over to Atlantic Records.

Jerry Wexler and I had had some preliminary conversations on the phone, but I had to deal with him in person. I needed to tell him, straight to his face, that Atlantic wasn't doing shit for me. I wanted Atlantic's best writer-producers, Leiber and Stoller, the guys who did the Drifters and Ben E. King, to work with me.

Jerry Wexler was gracious and saw me right away. He was a highly articulate guy with a sincere manner. He gave me a great deal of time while his partner, Ahmet Ertegun, ignored me.

"Sorry about West," Wexler said. "I like Robert. I hope you've been able to get new representation."

"I'm here representing myself, Mr. Wexler," I said. "You're not promoting me right. You're not recording me right, and you're also not producing me right."

"What do you suggest?" he asked.

"I want Leiber and Stoller. I feel their songs. I could have hits with Leiber and Stoller."

"Leiber and Stoller are no longer with us," said Wexler. "They formed their own label, Red Bird. But I have another writer-producer who I think is right for you."

"Who?"

"Burt Bacharach. He did 'Don't Make Me Over' for Dionne Warwick."

"I don't like the song. Too lightweight. I need gutsier writers like Leiber and Stoller."

"They're gone, and I can't bring 'em back."

"Then I'm gone," I said. "Everyone says I've been on Atlantic long enough."

"You sure you want to do this, Bettye?"

"Damn sure."

"You want to go out there alone, with no manager or label."

"I don't feel like you're all that interested in me as an artist," I said. "If you were, you'd get me another record right away."

He mentioned Burt Bacharach again. I couldn't imagine singing his kind of fluffy song.

"I need to be free right now," I said. "I need you to tear up my Atlantic contract because it's not making either of us any money."

"Tell you what, Bettye," said Wexler. "I'll tear up this contract, but then I'm gonna write you a check for five hundred dollars."

"For what?"

"Just because you're going to need it. No strings attached, just a little money from a record man who worries that you're gonna find it very goddamn cold out there."

Little did I know that Jerry Wexler was right. It wasn't just cold, it was fuckin' freezing.

I went to the hospital to see Robert West. He didn't look good. Katherine confirmed what I'd already been told. It wasn't clear whether he'd ever recover. I had to move on.

The next move was easy. I went to see the only other person I knew in New York—Frank Kocian, the accountant for Shaw Artists Corporation, the outfit that booked me. As it happened, Frank was fed up with accounting and eager to manage. He had eyes to manage me. He took me to dinner and, straight up, asked if I wanted a professional *and* personal relationship. Professional was good enough for me, and Frank proved to be a gentleman.

He showed me New York City—the Apollo, the Palm Café, and the Baby Grand, where he got me a gig. When someone said, "I wouldn't leave Harlem to go to heaven," I understood. The Baby Grand was the kind of club I'd read about in *Jet*. Nipsey Russell was closing just as I was opening. Anyone might come through the door—Joe Louis, Sugar Ray Robinson, Adam Clayton Powell. This was Harlem, baby!

Sometime after my appearance at the Baby Grand, Frank Kocian took me to Small's Paradise at 135th Street and Seventh Avenue. Walking through the door, I was smacked in the face by a familiar sound—"Whoa, whoa, ah whoa, whoa . . . need your lovin' every day." It was Don Gardner and Dee Dee Ford singing the hell out of their hit "I Need Your Lovin'." Dee Dee was on organ and Don on drums, blasting the kind of full-powered rhythm-and-blues I saw as my specialty. These were people who would appreciate me.

They did, and just like that, I found a home in a hip Harlem club. I was especially grateful to be hired as a singer because both Don and Dee Dee were superb singers themselves. The last thing they needed was another vocalist.

Don was a doll. He came up in Philly with Jimmy Smith, where they'd formed a trio. It was Don who had Jimmy switch from piano to organ, thus changing the course of jazz history. Jimmy would gain greater fame, but Don's musicianship was just as stupendous. Like a true master, he floated effortlessly from genre to genre—bop, doo-wop, R&B, you name it. Don could write, arrange, sing, and play drums. It burns me up that most histories of American music make no mention of Don Gardner. In my book, he's a giant. And beyond his crazy chops, he was a wonderful human being.

Dee Dee was different. She was supertalented—a terrific writer, singer, and organist, but insecurities ruled her mind. She was long and lanky with skinny arms and oversize feet. Long and lanky would have been cool if Twiggy had been popular, but Twiggy hadn't yet arrived. Dee Dee helped me out with music and I helped her out cosmetically. I tweezed her eyebrows and put her in a blond wig. She started looking good and gaining confidence. Unfortunately, she used her newfound sex appeal to go after our trumpet player, a gay brother. When the brother came out, Dee Dee was devastated. Dee Dee lived in a state of emotional high drama.

I witnessed some high drama of my own the night an old lady came in the club wrapped in a blanket. She looked homeless. She was wearing hospital-issued paper shoes and a tattered hat with a feather sticking out. Patrons of the club knew who she was and coaxed her to get up and do a song. I had never seen her before and was not thrilled about her singing in my domain. But I had no choice. The people wanted to hear her, and the people were right. Tearing into the song "Candy," she was so strong, so frighteningly soulful that the customers wouldn't let me on for my second set. It was disgraceful, but it was exactly what should have happened to my eighteen-year-old arrogant self. Out of ignorance, I had not recognized Big Maybelle. If you're Big Maybelle, you don't get strung out on heroin, live in doorways, and get your career denied for twenty-five years so some little bitch with a big booty can come in and kick your ass. Maybelle kicked *my* ass—and with good reason.

Not only was Small's Paradise my longest-lasting New York performing home, it also became my school for life lessons. The first involved Esther Phillips, whom I'd been hearing since I was a little girl. Esther had an up-and-down career. She was a big R&B star in the fifties, but she was struggling in the sixties. When I saw her at Small's, she was hanging out with Erma Franklin, Aretha's big sister. Unlike her far more challenging sibling, Erma was a sweetheart.

Esther had been drinking that night and getting high. She and Erma were wearing their little mink coats. I hadn't gotten mine yet, but I was eager to do so. New York is cold in the winter. I joined them at the bar, and men started buying us drinks. We were chitchatting up a storm when suddenly Esther falls into a junkie nod. Her eyeballs disappear, her head sinks down, and her big fat lower lip practically hangs on the bar. She looks like a derelict. Now, I'm all for drinking hard and getting high. I like wine, weed, and cocaine. But if this is what heroin does to you, I want no part of it. My need to look good is greater than my need for a drug with a bigger bang. No way am I gonna let myself go like that. Esther provided a compelling countermodel of what I did *not* want to be. And no matter how far out there I ventured, heroin was never part of my life.

Image was. There was never a time, no matter how high or low I might have been, that I didn't want to look good. When I got to New York, I found an apartment over a beauty salon and became friends with the owner, Wilbert, a sweet old queen. At the time, gay hadn't exploded as a public thing. I thought all gays were young and was astounded to meet an older homosexual. Wilbert was the one who fashioned some wigs for me in a color he called LaVette Blond. It was perfectly blended to enhance my skin tone. Etta James was still lurking around as a blond, and because I loved everything Etta did, I had to go blond as well. Wilbert sculpted that wig with all the finesse of Michelangelo. When I looked in the mirror, I was thrilled. I couldn't get over myself. I also couldn't get over how Wilbert had been living with his sixty-five-year-old boyfriend for thirty years. His boyfriend looked like a high school principal. These were dignified gentlemen.

"Sissies come in all flavors," Wilbert said to me with a good-natured laugh.

Yes, sir, I was learning all sorts of things in the big city.

One of the first things I learned was the severity of my mistake in leaving Atlantic. I couldn't interest another label. So when I spotted Luther Dixon walking down Broadway, I was excited. These were the days when all the girl singers were looking for a producer husband. And all of us were looking for Luther. He was a fantastic writer, a guy who'd composed for everyone from Perry Como to Bobby Darin to Elvis to Jimmy Reed. Luther was the creative power behind Florence Greenberg and Scepter Records, where the Shirelles had broken the bank. A little later, Luther would marry Inez Foxx, famous for "Mockingbird," her duo with her brother, Charlie, but when I saw Luther walking down Broadway that day, he was a free man.

"Bettye," he said. "What are you doing in New York, baby?"

"Working at Small's Paradise."

"You recording right now?"

"No, I'm not."

"You interested in going into the studio?"

"You know I am."

"Got a track that might work for you. Come with me and let's see if you pick up the melody. If it works out, I'll take it to Florence. If she likes it, we'll release it as a single. Cool?"

"Cool."

Cutting it was strange. I had never sung over a track. I was used to live men playing their instruments behind me. I liked the excitement of their proximity. No matter, I did what I had to do. Luther liked it and said he'd get back to me with Florence's reaction. He never did. I never saw him again, I never saw Florence. Twenty-five years passed before I heard another word about the song. It wasn't until the nineties when a British label said they'd gone through the Scepter vaults and found this song by me.

"What's it called?" I asked.

"'Happiness Will Only Cost You One Thin Dime.'"

The title didn't immediately ring a bell, and when they played it, I wasn't even sure that it was me singing.

"If it's not me," I told the English guys, "we need to find this bitch."

After repeated listenings, I did recognize my voice and remembered the Luther Dixon episode.

A far more memorable recording from the mid-sixties was something I was sure was a hit. Frank Kocian introduced me to Nate McCalla, whose underworld contacts bankrolled Calla Records. Frank convinced Nate to put me on his label. Musically, the pieces seemed to be coming together. Personally, though, things were not great.

I was living with a barber who was a drug dealer and a hustler. My friend Dee Dee Ford was still in love with the gay trumpet player. This is the background to her writing "Let Me Down

Easy," a song that, for legal reasons, Dee Dee wrote under the name "Wreich-Holloway." Don Gardner produced the session and we were lucky to get Dale Warren, a Detroit arranger who'd worked with the Supremes, to write the chart. It was a mournful thing. It was a soulful thing. I was nineteen when I recorded it, but people said I sounded thirty. It came out in 1965, the year Marvin had "Ain't That Peculiar" and the Temps had "My Girl." "Let Me Down Easy" did reach number 20 on the R&B chart but then vanished in a flash. Some of that fault might have been mine.

McCalla and his cronies loved me. They gave me an unlimited budget to promote the song. They asked, "What TV show you want to go on?" With their muscle, I had many choices. I said *Shindig!* 'cause that was the only show I knew. If I had been smart like Berry Gordy, I would have said *The Ed Sullivan Show*. Sullivan was the big reason why the Motown acts crossed over in such spectacular fashion. But, still a teenager, I had my mind on teenage shows.

My appearance on *Shindig!* no doubt helped "Let Me Down Easy" from going down too fast. I'd call it a minor hit, but I still think of it as a major song. Nearly a half-century later, I'm still singing the muthafucka and feeling the truth of the message.

I was singing the song at the Regal Theater in Chicago, on the same bill with the Dells, the Radiants, and Marvin Gaye. I saw this as my chance to finally catch Marvin. When it came to approaching women, Marvin always looked like a frightened lamb, but I vowed to be gentle enough to make him comfortable. After we had lunch one day, I invited him to my room, but he never came. After dinner the next day, I invited him again, and again he didn't show. On the last night of the run, I gave up and decided to have a party. Chuck Barksdale of the Dells showed up as well as deejay Pervis Spann. A lot of people were squeezed into my room. We were raucous and loud and having a large time when I heard a knock on the door. When I opened it to see who was there, I could have fainted—Marvin!

"Oh," he said, "I thought you'd be alone." And with that he turned and walked away.

Marvin had finally come for me, and I blew it. I'd lost a once-in-a-lifetime opportunity. I'm still kicking myself.

The deepest truth, though, was that New York, for all its thrills, hadn't given me what I'd sought. In my mind, I had come to the city as a star. Before I got there, I was being billed above Otis Redding. Now, with "I've Been Loving You Too Long" and "Respect," Otis was a much bigger star. I had had so much respect for myself that I told a big shot like Jerry Wexler I didn't need Atlantic. Now the song I was singing was called "Let Me Down Easy," and believe me, I was singing to myself.

At the same time, I can't look back and cast myself as a depressive. It's one thing to have the blues. I think I've had the blues—musically and otherwise—most of my life. But having the blues is different from depression. To me, depression connotes despair. Living in New York during the mid-sixties, I was not in despair. I always thought the big break was around the corner. I always knew I could sing. And besides, the city was a wondrous place, filled with characters who never ceased to excite my imagination.

The city was hard-edged, but it also had some soft corners. And if survival meant finding a way to take off the edge by finding those corners, I was determined to do so. I was sure I could survive in New York.

And I was sure wrong.

Groupies Who Sang

Tammi Montgomery and Yvonne Fair had much in common. They were singers who had both been with James Brown, onstage and in bed. Like me, they loved being around singing stars and pimp-producers to whom they gave up their love easily and often. We were essentially groupies who sang.

I first met Yvonne when I opened for James Brown. She had a single, "I Found You," that James recut himself. It came out as "I Got You (I Feel Good)" and turned into one of his biggest hits. Yvonne had a strong voice and carefree attitude. In contrast, Tammi had a coy voice and a hard-core attitude. I met her before she changed her name to Tammi Terrell and left James for David Ruffin and Motown.

I was in my dressing room, angry that I'd been told that James Brown didn't want me to close my set with "Let Me Down Easy," because I was getting too much applause. Compared with James's more outrageous dictatorial tirades, this was nothing. Everyone around James was afraid of him. I wasn't. I was ready to challenge him, but I was barred from seeing him. I never got to register my complaint. I respected James's music, but on a personal level, I saw him as an especially ignorant man.

I was feeling especially disrespected when my dressing room door burst open and Tammi Montgomery was standing there.

"All right, bitch," she said, "I know you been looking for me."

She pulled up her skirt and grabbed a handgun wedged against her garter belt.

I laughed.

"I ain't been looking for you, bitch," I said. "I don't even know why you're here."

She told me she'd been hearing my records and wanted me to know she could outsing me any day of the week. I didn't argue. Only a fool argues with a gun.

Seeing I was as sassy as she was, she put the gun away and declared peace. We wound up liking each other. Tammi was a free spirit, and in that sense we were sisters. A couple of years later as Tammi Terrell, she wound her voice around Marvin's on those beautiful duets. I appreciated the subtlety of her singing. Of all Marvin's duet partners—Mary Wells, Kim Weston, Diane Ross—Tammi was the most engaging. When she died of a brain tumor in 1970, she was only twenty-four.

The notion of the groupie/singer helps explain why Tammi, Yvonne, and I did the things we did. Diane Ross undoubtedly also fits into that category. Even though we were semi-stars ourselves, we were so enamored of the stars that we'd use every feminine charm at our command to win our way into their world. Beyond the sheer delight of being in the company of magnificent artists like Marvin Gaye or David Ruffin, we knew that we needed to be more than good singers. We needed men to sponsor our cause. We knew that they liked hearing us sing. But we also knew that if they enjoyed sex with us, they'd help our careers.

Other men, who were not magnificent artists, also led us to believe that they could help our careers. Ray Scott was one such man. He was a comic and sometime singer who became obsessed with me. His comedy was modeled after Redd Foxx's. He wasn't as funny as Redd, but funny enough to gig at the Baby Grand, which is where I met him. His true talent was pimping. Ray had a fleet of white girls working for him. He was a dog, but a super-cool, slick New York dog. He had a boatload of high-octane cocaine that he was always coaxing me to try. But his coaxing didn't stop with drugs.

Ray was salacious. He loved whispering to me, "Why don't you do him?" Or, "Why don't you do both those guys?" None of those promptings motivated me. I've never been into sex with strangers. But Ray's sex obsession didn't end there. He liked to put together what he considered freaky combinations.

I remember the night I had gone to the Apollo to see my friends the Majors, the group produced by Jerry Ragovoy. They had a little hit called "A Wonderful Dream." One of the Majors introduced me to his girlfriend, Cynthia Wharton, a stunning woman. I was getting ready to hang out at the Baby Grand and suggested everyone join me. The Majors were too tired, but Cynthia, whom I called Cindy, came along.

Ray Scott was at the club, and the minute he saw Cindy, he said, "Why don't you fuck her? I think you'd both love it. But if you do, one word of advice—don't let her get on top."

I laughed off the remark, but the thought stayed with me. I

can't say that I was longing to make love to a woman. Yet the idea was not unappealing, especially with someone as lovely as Cindy. She was another groupie extraordinaire. She knew every black singer, dancer, comic, and actor in New York and was welcome at every backstage, slipping in and out of limousines with the grace of a cat. If groupies had formed a union, Cindy would have been our president.

The provocation of the pimp, who began giving money to both Cindy and me, fueled my motivation. Those pimps loved to watch girls have sex. They also loved jumping into bed with two women. Had Ray not insisted on it and stoked the fire with copious amounts of cocaine, none of this might have happened. But it did, and I liked it. I liked it well enough that Cindy was in my life for the next thirty years. We'd have our boyfriends and husbands. We'd live our separate lives, but if we were in the same city on the same night, we'd get together.

My dalliances with women just sort of happened. I've never had hang-ups about sex, an area where I've felt fortunately free. In the case of women, once the sex was over, it was over. It never turned to romance. The friendship with Cindy, though, remained strong. She and I had some wild adventures.

A member of one of the major singing groups—I don't want to embarrass him by using his name—was madly in love with me but too shy to make a move. He was adorable. I can't say I loved him, but I appreciated his attention. One night I asked if he wanted to come back to the hotel with me and Cindy. He did. When we got there, Cindy and I started getting it on. Naturally, the guy was welcome to join in, but he was terrified. He just stood there and watched, his shirt buttoned up to his neck, tears running down his cheeks. We wondered what the other guys in the group would say if they knew he had two naked broads up in bed and all he could do was cry. I never could coax him to join us, but that just shows how sex affects everyone differently.

Don't get the idea that men were the only pimps. They certainly dominated the field, but there were women who also played the role. Take Doris Troy. She had scored a top-ten pop hit in 1963, "Just One Look," as a singer and cowriter. Doris was the first person I met who lived on Central Park West, a fancy address, where she liked to give parties attended by entertainers. I was flattered to be invited into her little group. Every time I went up to Doris's place, though, I noticed a bevy of beautiful women. Doris was either matching them up with men who came to look them over or sending them on the streets to find johns on their own. Doris was not only an effective singer, but an effective businesswoman. Some of the male pimps felt threatened, but they knew not to threaten Doris. She was bad.

As a pimp, Doris was cool, but Ted White was the coolest. And when he called to say he and Aretha were in New York and he wanted to see me, I eagerly went to their suite at the Americana Hotel. The three of us spent the afternoon blowing cocaine—Ted's cocaine. I rarely carried drugs. I never had to. They were usually extended to me by generous hosts and suitors.

I have no idea whether Aretha knew that Ted and I occasionally had sex. Given how close I was to him, she may have assumed so. On the other hand, Ted may have kept her in the dark. Either way, we didn't have problems getting high together and shooting the breeze. With Ted present, Aretha let him do all the talking.

He told me how Jerry Wexler at Atlantic had offered Aretha a contract. They were frustrated with her current label, Columbia, because she had not enjoyed any major hits. He thought that Wexler had a good understanding of singers like me and Aretha.

"Well," I said, "Aretha will tell you that we're not all that much alike. Aretha is church, and I ran from the church. Besides, her church is Baptist and mine was Catholic."

"You're both rhythm-and-blues singers who can sing anything," said Ted. "The challenge is to find what that 'anything' is. Look what Wexler did for Otis and Wilson Pickett."

"That's right," I said, "but look what Aretha did on that 'Skylark' song she cut for Columbia. She killed it."

"Thanks," said Aretha, who was not inclined to disagree with anything her husband said.

Aretha was comfortable with me, not only because she saw me as a colleague, but because she knew I had hung with her sister Erma. For years Aretha's baby sister, Carolyn, and brother Cecil shared the same drug dealer with me. They were more extroverted than Aretha, who in those years was the quiet one. Even high, she was shy. I asked her about some records she had made with Clyde Otis like *Runnin' Out of Fools*. All she said was that she enjoyed working with Clyde and thought he was a good writer. I remember that Jim Lewis had told me that Otis had produced Sarah Vaughan's only pop hit, "Broken Hearted Melody." He'd also been responsible for the smash duets with Dinah Washington and Brook Benton.

"Clyde's cool," said Ted, "but a little behind the curve. We're trying to get ahead of the curve."

"I've been trying to do the same thing myself."

"I like your 'Let Me Down Easy,'" said Aretha.

"Thanks," I said, "but it's hardly paying the rent."

There was a knock on the door. Room service. Ted put away the blow and we nibbled on cheese and sipped champagne. The mood was cordial. I asked Aretha about Teddy, her son with Ted. Back in Detroit, many were the times I'd been with Ted and Teddy. I felt like I was part of Ted White's extended family. In those days, it was not unusual for wives of pimps to socialize with both their employees and girlfriends.

But then again, Ted *was* unusual. He groomed women in many walks of life. He got involved in their careers and stayed involved. I've no doubt he could be violent, but he was never that way with me.

Clarence Paul sent me a ticket to go home to Detroit. During that visit, Clarence had an idea for a party that he wanted to host in my blue basement bedroom. Stevie Wonder was turning sixteen, and Clarence was convinced it was time the boy became a man. Who did I think was the right woman?

"He deserves the best," I said.

"I'm not volunteering you," said Clarence.

"I'm not worthy of that honor. Marrie Early is. If you want to initiate Stevie in an unforgettable way, you need Marrie. There could be no more beautiful birthday gift than Marrie Early."

"Can't argue with that," said Clarence. "I'll call her."

I got the food and drinks, the friends and the music. I decorated my basement with balloons. When Stevie arrived with Clarence, he walked down the stairs to the basement and bumped his head on the low ceiling. He was excited. Clarence might have told him about the special gift that awaited him.

We had a blast, but sadly, Marrie never arrived. I know she was eager to do the honors, but something else more pressing must have come up. We were all disappointed, and no one more so than Stevie.

Back in New York, my life was anchored by my gig at Small's Paradise with Don and Dee Dee. Dee Dee was also my buddy. One day we were riding around the city when two guys in a convertible pulled up beside us. We started flirting, and one thing led to another. I went off with one of the guys, a big-time drug dealer. Although he already had a wife and a girlfriend, he took a liking to me and vice versa.

Meanwhile, Dee Dee's romantic fortunes continued to decline. She fell into a deep depression. There was a period when I was working an out-of-town gig and gave her my clothes for safekeeping. At the time, she was staying with Margherite Mays, Willie Mays's ex-wife, on Long Island. But poor Dee Dee. The blues got the best of her and she burned down the place. All my clothes, along with most everything else, went up in smoke.

My new boyfriend was good enough to replace them. He obviously took our relationship seriously because when he caught me with another man, he cut up all the clothes he had bought me, including six pairs of shoes. I had never seen anyone cut up shoes before. When I asked him why, given that he had a wife *and* a mistress in addition to me, he would feel so betrayed, he was too angry to answer.

"I'm not even number two," I said. "I'm number three. Number three gets to fool around a little."

"Not on me she doesn't."

Well, if I thought this guy was obsessive and possessive when it came to women, I hadn't seen anything yet. The next man to enter my life was in a category all his own.

J

It astounds me that I succumbed to a muthafucka like J, the name I'm giving to the man you met at the beginning of this book. He represented the end of my venture in New York City. He also represented one of the low points of my life.

How in the world did it happen?

I was singing at Small's. As Stevie would later say, I was living for the city. I found a way to survive; I even had a little following. My second single for the gangsters at Calla, "Only Your Love Can Save Me," didn't save me at all. Although it was written by Jo Armstead along with the team of Nick Ashford and Valerie Simpson—on the verge of writing smashes for Marvin and Tammi—the single sank like a lead balloon. My only income was a slim salary and the occasional tip from a drunk at the bar. When I met J, you could say I was vulnerable. But when it came to falling head over heels in love, I've always been vulnerable.

In my defense, the man was magnificent. Good looks in a man have often blinded me to his character. When I'd see a handsome guy showing interest in me, his stares of appreciation killed off my brain cells. All powers of scrutiny collapsed.

Later I learned that J had spent ten years in prison, but on the night we met, I saw not the slightest hint of criminality in his deep brown eyes. All I saw was sweetness and light. He dressed with the same sophistication as Ted White did. His speaking voice had the honey-coated tones of a midnight disc jockey. And there was the irresistibility of his high-toned culture.

J read me poems. J introduced me to haute cuisine. He knew the difference between northern and southern Italian cooking. He introduced me to Spanish paella and fine French wines. He cast a spell over me to the point that he convinced me to quit my job at Small's.

Don Gardner was aghast.

"I wouldn't do that if I were you," he said.

I didn't listen.

In my mind—my messed-up mind—I was thinking, *Well, at least I'm over Clarence Paul. It took a mighty man like J to finally get me to fall in love with someone other than Clarence.* But my thinking was wildly distorted. The distortion deepened when I took J home to meet Mama and Sister.

"Betty Jo," said Mama, "he's a fine-looking man."

"No man," said Sister, "has the right to be that pretty."

Obviously, they didn't push me into this relationship. I'd found J on my own. But they were as blind to his cruel side as I was.

For me to withdraw from my world of music and friends was an amazing thing. I'm a musical animal. I'm a social animal. I like to party. I like to hang at the clubs. I like to go out.

"Ain't no going out unless you going out *for* me or *with* me," said J.

Soon he was asking me, "Do you think you were smart before you met me?"

"Yes," I said.

"The hell you were. You were dumb." And with that, he slapped me across the face.

Who was he to talk to me like that? And who was I to accept that treatment? What was in my mind? What was in my heart?

J had a hooker I'll call Helen. She was his main earner, a stunning woman who worked with remarkable efficiency. She had perfected the art of turning tricks. She attracted men with money. So refined were her techniques that her tips were sometimes as big as her fees. Imagine the pleasure a man must feel to voluntarily double the fee he pays for sex.

Helen would often be in the Amsterdam Avenue apartment where I was living with J. She cooked and slaved over the man to a sickening degree.

One evening Helen spent hours cooking J a five-course dinner. When he sat down to eat, she sat next to him and, as though he were a child, cut up his food and, with her fork, put it in his mouth.

I laughed out loud. "That is some funny shit," I said. "That is some *ridiculous* shit."

J got up from the table, whacked me across my mouth, and snarled, "Shut up, bitch. No one asked you nothing."

In looking back at this sad period of my life, I can't help but ask myself what took me so long to leave this man. When he stopped me from seeing my friends or singing in public, why didn't I tell him to go fuck himself? After he ordered me out on the streets to turn tricks and told me not to come back until I earned a hundred dollars a day, why did I continue to do his bidding for another two or three months?

I was a great groupie, but a horrible hooker. My judgment was bad, my approach inept, my hustle pathetic. I only survived because of the kindness of Frank Kocian, who would give me a hundred from time to time. King Curtis helped me out. So did Don Gardner. Other musicians who started making money as pimps felt sorry for me and gave me enough to placate J. Then one day I ran into Luther Dixon.

"Bettye," he said, "you look tired, baby."

"I am."

"What are you up to?"

For whatever reasons, I told him the truth. The words just spilled out of my mouth. "I'm working for J," I said.

"Lord, have mercy," Luther sympathized. "That man's a monster. How much you gotta give him to keep from getting beat?"

"A hundred a day."

"Here's a hundred, just 'cause I don't wanna see you hurt."

He put the money in my hand and went on his way.

An hour later, I put the money in J's hand.

When I couldn't make my daily quota, sometimes I'd steal it from Helen. She was earning so much she never knew the difference.

When I walked past a record shop or turned on the radio, I'd hear hit after hit coming out of Detroit. These were friends of mine, people I'd grown up with—"Reach Out I'll Be There," "What Becomes of the Brokenhearted," "My World Is Empty Without You."

My world was empty *with* J. My world was hell. Better men

came through for me. Clarence Paul and Ted White would always wire me a hundred bucks so I could avoid another beating. But can you imagine how incredibly stupid I felt getting money from these guys so I could placate this raging asshole of a pimp?

I thought about the last two songs I'd recorded for Calla. The A-side was "I'm Just a Fool for You." Was there ever a more fitting title to describe my ridiculous situation with J? The B-side was "Stand Up Like a Man." It was when I was listening to that single that I finally saw the light. Enough was enough. I had to stand up like a woman. I can't tell you where the strength came from. It was not a religious epiphany. I didn't hear angels singing on high. I didn't hear the voice of God. All I heard were two words coming from my mouth to J's ears that should have been spoken months before.

"Fuck you."

I said that to his face. I told him I was going and there was nothing he could say to change my mind.

That's when he grabbed me and hung me over the edge of the building.

That's when I wiggled my way out of that perilous moment by calling his bluff.

That's when he let me go and, taking no chances, that's when I ran out, leaving all my worldly possessions with him.

I was on the streets, a shoeless twenty-year-old, broke and scared to death.

There could be no doubt—New York City had kicked my ass.

Time to tuck my tail between my legs and crawl home.

The Teacher

When Mama saw me walk through the door of our home on Trowbridge, she collapsed. She thought she had seen a ghost.

"Betty Jo," she finally found the strength to say, "you look like death warmed over."

I was a raggedy mess. I had these thin little pants, a cheap cotton blouse, and a pair of worn-out slippers. My hair was disheveled. At one point I must have had fifty wigs. Now I had none. I knew I needed help.

They say when the student is ready, the teacher will appear. Well, that certainly was the case with me. But given my headstrong personality, I didn't think I was ready to learn. No matter how badly New York had beaten me up, I came home with my know-it-all attitude undiminished. Fortunately, the teacher knew how to handle me. He was as hardheaded as I was. He taught me in spite of myself. He saved my professional life and prepared me for a future I was too shortsighted to see. He planted artistic seeds in my head and heart that took decades to flower.

This was Jim Lewis, the musician's-union man I'd met just before leaving for New York.

"Thought you swore you weren't ever coming back," he said when he saw me at the Chit Chat Lounge.

"That was my intention."

"And what happened?"

"New York was a little rough."

"A little rough?" he asked suspiciously.

"Okay, a lot rough."

"So you came home to get that training you need."

"What kind of training are you talking about?"

"Singing training. History training."

"What kind of history?"

"History of the singers who can teach you a thing or two about singing. You ever listen to Billie Holiday?"

"I don't like her."

"You're showing your ignorance, girl."

"You're getting on my nerves."

"Just take my card. When you come to your senses, give me a call."

I took his card, swearing I'd never call him and figuring I wouldn't have to. He'd call me.

Returning home wasn't easy. Admitting defeat never is. But if you're really a singer, you gotta sing. Your need to sing is greater than your pride. You sing whenever and wherever you can—and that's just what I did.

Many of the Motown people didn't even know I'd been gone. They were absorbed in Berry Gordy's ever-expanding empire. If I had had a smash in New York, they might have taken note. And while "Let Me Down Easy" made some noise, it was not enough to get the attention of my Detroit friends riding high with number-one pop hits.

Of the Motown singers, I was closest to the two I considered the best—David Ruffin and Marvin Gaye. And because Marvin was aligned with Clarence Paul, I was with him often.

While Marvin's marriage to Anna Gordy got him into the Gordy family, he was never happy with either his wife or his wife's brother, boss Berry. The Marvin I knew was submissive and easily intimidated. Anna pushed his career and got him into the recording studio when no one else could. But, as everyone in Detroit knew, she was also involved with other men.

Diane Ross played the Motown game with more skill than any girl up there. She slept her way up the Motown command, beginning with Smokey, Berry's first lieutenant and best friend. Then she moved on to Brian Holland, one-third of the Holland-Dozier-Holland team that was writing and producing the Supremes' hits. Most of the female singers felt the same way about Diane as I did. We saw her as a stuck-up bitch with a small voice and big ambition. So it was with special delight that we witnessed her comeuppance.

It happened at the 20 Grand, a sophisticated Detroit club where the Motowners met after hours. I was there with Martha Reeves. She and her Vandellas were riding high. At the adjoining table were Brian Holland and Diane Ross. At about two a.m., the mellow evening suddenly got messy when Brian's wife, Sharon, came storming in. Mrs. Holland was no shrinking violet. She pointed to Brian and screamed, "You, get in the goddamn car." Brian jumped up and did as he was told. "And you," said Sharon, pointing to Diane, "I'm gonna kick your scrawny ass."

With amazement and delight, Martha and I watched Sharon beat down Diane with such thoroughness, tearing off her clothes with such ferocity, that America's Supreme sweetheart was left standing in her slip, panties, and bra.

If I had been smarter, I would have modeled myself after Diane, who reached the summit by screwing Berry and having his baby. Instead, I chose Clarence Paul, a man with limited influence. Clarence's clique, which included his partner, Morris Broadnax, was on the outside looking in. The Paul–Broadnax team had molded Stevie. They got him going. Together with Stevie they wrote "Until You Come Back to Me (That's What I'm Gonna Do)," which became a hit for Aretha. But it was really Sylvia Moy and Hank Cosby who took Stevie into the stratosphere. Together with Stevie's own critical contribution, they were the main forces behind "Uptight (Everything's Alright)," "I Was Made to Love Her," "My Cherie Amour," and "Signed, Sealed, Delivered I'm Yours," the songs that turned Stevie into a superstar. Clarence, however, never moved up into that first tier.

I know you're crazy for Clarence Paul," said Jim Lewis, when he called me for a date. He didn't hide the fact of his marriage, nor did he hide his desire to fuck me.

"Clarence and I are close," was all I said.

"If you want to run with the Motown crowd, you picked the wrong horse."

"I can live without that crowd."

"But haven't you ever wondered, given how you can just about outsing anyone over there, why Berry has never approached you?"

"That's just it. He doesn't want me to outsing his stars."

"Don't be stupid," said Jim. "Berry's a businessman. The more successful the stars he signs, the more money for him. No, it isn't that he doesn't know about your talent. It's that he doesn't like your man Clarence. He's blacklisted Clarence and anyone associated with him."

"I don't believe it."

"Then you're blind. Look how Holland-Dozier-Holland has taken off. Look at the money Mickey Stevenson has made. Is Clarence seeing that kind of money? I don't think so. Look, I know Berry well. As a union rep, I'm in touch with him all the time. He's a smart guy and a brilliant salesman, but he can also be vindictive. He's not a guy you wanna cross."

"And you think Clarence crossed him?"

"Clarence got in early. Given his talent, he should be wielding real power over there. But he can't even get you a deal on Motown, can he?"

There was no arguing with that.

I later confronted Clarence with Jim's theory.

"Jim thinks Berry is holding you back. He thinks Berry has something against you. Is that true, Clarence?"

"The only thing I can think of," he said, "was this time we were all at the 20 Grand. Ray was there without Berry."

Ray was Berry's second wife, the one who had been instrumental in helping him start Motown.

"What happened?" I asked.

"Ray got drunk and didn't have a ride. So I took her home. She invited me in and poured us some cognac. We blew some coke and the next thing I knew I was out."

"Did you fuck her?"

"No."

"Then what was the problem?"

"Berry. When he got home later that night, Ray and I were both laid out on the floor, naked."

"But you said you didn't fuck her."

"I didn't."

"Then why in hell were the two of you naked?"

"I can't say. All I know is that we'd been blowing cocaine."

"And to blow coke, you gotta get naked?"

"That's the part that doesn't make sense."

"And Berry believed you when you said you didn't fuck his wife?"

"Berry was plenty pissed."

"And you think he's held that against you?"

"I guess there's a chance of that."

"You *guess*! Think about it, Clarence—the man walks in and sees you and Ray naked on the floor."

"But he isn't even seeing Ray anymore. They broke up long ago."

"What difference does that make, Clarence? Husbands don't forget shit like that. *Ever.*"

Clarence would never leave his wife for me, but he'd also never give up on me. Before Frank Kocian gave up on the music business, he began a little label called Big Wheel. I cut a couple of songs that Clarence had written. The first, "Tears in Vain," had already been recorded by Stevie as well as the Supremes. Clarence composed the second, "I'm Holding On," a good description of my dwindling career, with Morris Broadnax, a consummate writer. Nax's lyrics for Marvin's "When I'm Alone I Cry" are among the most beautiful in Motown history. In my own history, Nax never stopped hitting on me. I'd cry on his shoulder about how Clarence didn't love me, only to have him say, "But Bettye LaVette, I do. Why mess with Clarence when you can have me?"

"Nax," I said, "you're betraying your best friend."

"For you," he answered, "I'd betray God in heaven."

"Put it in a song, Nax. 'Cause you sure ain't putting it in me."

The Big Wheel songs died a painful death. Maybe it was their lack of success that made me a little more receptive to Jim Lewis's continual campaign to not only manage me but train me as well.

In 1967, Jim and I became lovers. I was twenty-one and he was forty-five, a happily married man happy to have a hot little thing on the side. He was also sincere about teaching me the art of singing.

"It's not an art," I told him one day, as we were driving around Detroit, "it's a natural-born talent."

At that very moment, Sarah Vaughan was coming on the radio with her version of "I've Got a Crush on You."

"What would you call this?" he asked as he turned up the volume.

"I don't like it," I said. "She's oversinging."

He slammed on the brakes, turned to me, and barked, "Get out of the car."

"What are you talking about?"

"You're not gonna talk about Sarah Vaughan that way. Not in my car. Your ignorance is exceeded only by your arrogance."

And the man put me out. Good thing I was only five blocks away from my house.

The next week, though, we were back at it. Jim's passion for female singing was so deep that he required a protégé. He needed someone to teach. I needed someone who could get me gigs. Jim was that guy. His union position afforded him all sorts of opportunities to hire a singer for meetings, banquets, conventions, and political rallies. I also began to see that I did, in fact, need his training. His insistence that I learn my craft was strong enough to crack my arrogance. Jim was one of the few men who could get me to shut up.

"Have you heard of Anita O'Day?" he asked.

"No," I said.

"Well, you need to. She started out as a big band canary with Gene Krupa. Most of the great singers had big band experience. Ella with Chick Webb, Billie with Basie and Artie Shaw, Sarah with Earl Hines and Billy Eckstine, Dinah with Lionel Hampton."

He played me Anita's vocal on "Let Me Off Uptown," done with the Krupa band and trumpeter Roy Eldridge.

"She phrases like a horn player," I said.

"That's the point," said Jim. "That's the paradox. The best horn players—Coleman Hawkins and Lester Young and Johnny Hodges—model themselves after singers. They sing through their horns. And the best singers use their voices like instruments.

Listen to this record Anita made fifteen years later with Oscar Peterson. Listen to how she phrases as brilliantly as Oscar, the most brilliant pianist since Art Tatum."

"This jazz talk is wearing me out," I said.

"This jazz technique is what's going to let you sing in any style you choose. It's going to give you class and freedom. Listen to how freely Betty Carter sings. She also started out with Hampton. She was the girl singer and Little Jimmy Scott was the boy singer. Have you heard them?"

"No."

"Well, you will now."

Jim put on records by Carter and Scott. Betty sang like Charlie Parker played, fast and frenetic, while Jimmy hung back far behind the beat.

"Now listen to Betty's duets with Ray Charles," said Jim.

I still wasn't crazy about Betty, but I could hear why Jim considered Ray the absolute master.

"Here's a man," he explained, "who began by doing flat-out imitations of Charles Brown and Nat Cole. He was singing a kind of cocktail blues, very correct and yet intimate. Then he breaks out with his rhythm-and-blues stuff—'I Got a Woman,' 'What'd I Say.' And then, just when everyone considers him the best gospel/soul singer ever, he hits with country—'I Can't Stop Loving You.' In between, he's singing standards—'Am I Blue?'—and, just for good measure, has pop hits with 'Georgia on My Mind' and 'Ruby.' The reason Ray is such an important model for you, Bettye, is because, like you, he's a rough-and-tumble soul singer at heart. But that doesn't mean he's restricted to that category. His base is soul, but tenderness and sensitivity allow him to go all over the map. He makes any material his own. That's your goal."

When Jim talked about Ray, he made sense. I related to Ray, but I still had problems relating to Ella, who did not reach me emotionally, and Billie, whose poignant and pained delivery I appreciated only years later.

Jim's lessons kept coming. He schooled me on Gloria Lynne and considered her "I Wish You Love" a masterpiece. He insisted that I study Dakota Staton and Nancy Wilson. "Nancy," he said, "is the female version of Jimmy Scott." He made sure I ignored none of the white singers. Beyond Anita O'Day, he had me listening to June Christy, Chris Connor, Peggy Lee, Jo Stafford, Julie London, Jeri Southern. "Listen to their intonation," he said. "Hear how they enunciate, how they never cut off the word before the meaning is clear. It's all about storytelling."

Jim considered Carmen McRae a great storyteller. "She listened to Billie," he said. "Billie listened to Bessie and Louis, so when you hear Carmen you hear a whole chunk of history."

After that little lecture, he started making me sing songs like "The Man That Got Away."

"Judy Garland?" I asked.

"Hell, yes, Judy Garland," he answered. "Judy Garland is brilliant."

After Judy, it was Sinatra. After Sinatra, Tony Bennett. After Tony, Johnny Hartman. The list kept growing. After a while, the list was just too damn long.

"Your lessons are getting on my nerves," I told Jim.

Jim's response was always the same: "Just listen. Keep listening."

I listened to Helen Humes, Lena Horne, Arthur Prysock, Irene Reid, Joe Williams, Rosemary Clooney, Jon Hendricks,

Bill Henderson, and Shirley Horn, who sang as far back behind the beat as Little Jimmy Scott.

Hour after hour, week after week, month after month—listening, listening, listening, with Jim pointing out every last nuance of every single song sung by every singer.

These free lessons were blessings, though at first I saw them as burdens. I was shortsighted.

"Whatever happens with your recording career," Jim was quick to say, "the techniques I'm showing you will allow you to sing professionally for the rest of your life. Study them carefully and you'll become a master."

Five years had passed since "My Man." I had suffered the humiliation of New York. I had recorded other singles and, other than the slim success of "Let Me Down Easy," none of them had hit. And while humility was not—and will never be—central to my character, I was forced to admit the truth: My Motown friends had become national stars while I was back home playing Phelps Lounge.

That's why Jim Lewis's confidence meant a lot. If he, with his encyclopedic knowledge of music, thought I was good enough to be great, I could tame my cockiness and listen to the man. It wasn't easy. I wasn't happy being told what to do. But his notions of how to phrase a lyric, how to present myself onstage, how to feel my way through all the genres, how to learn the standards—even the toughest ones like Billy Strayhorn's "Lush Life" and Thelonious Monk's "'Round Midnight"—were too sensible to deny. Besides, the beauty of the singers he loved best was finally breaking down my hardheaded defiance and warming my heart.

As I came of age, I was slowly becoming a different kind of

singer. My early education had been strictly in the streets. Now a teacher had come along, sat me down, and got me to pay attention to a legacy that he considered critical to my artistic development.

"Artistic development?" I asked. "Who the hell thinks about something like that?"

"Hardly anyone," Jim answered. "But hardly anyone ever grows in this business. If you want to grow, you've got to develop. Either that or you die."

I didn't want to die. I just wanted another hit.

Higher and Higher

It would be hard to argue that 1967 wasn't the hottest year in the hottest decade in the history of R&B. Ted White proved to be right in putting Aretha on Atlantic. Jerry Wexler became her producer and her first single, "I Never Loved a Man (The Way I Love You)," set her career soaring. Not many months later, she was on the cover of *Time* while I was considering slitting my wrists for not covering Otis Redding's "Respect" before she did. In years to come, I'd have many more wrist-slitting moments.

Of course, I was the one who told Wexler to get lost while Ted was smart enough to get Jerry into the studio with Aretha. Wexler had the right feel for tough-minded rhythm-and-blues in a way that Aretha's original producer, John Hammond, did not. Jerry was also the reigning king of the Muscle Shoals scene where the rhythm section, funky and loose, gave Aretha exactly the support she needed.

Other Detroiters, friends who'd been scuffling with me, were also enjoying sensational success. Martha and her Vandellas had "Jimmy Mack" and the Supremes had "Love Is Here and Now You're Gone." Little Stevie, produced by Sylvia Moy and Hank Cosby—not my man Clarence Paul—went number one with "I Was Made to Love Her." Jackie Wilson, the Detroiter we singers admired most, came out with his last smash hit, "(Your Love Keeps Lifting Me) Higher and Higher." The Motown producer I couldn't stand—the nasty, bad-tempered, overly aggressive Norman Whitfield—had "I Heard It Through the Grapevine" with Gladys Knight & the Pips. Norman was as brilliant as he was hateful. A year later, Marvin would also go number one with "Grapevine" and have Whitfield hits with "That's the Way Love Is" and "Too Busy Thinking About My Baby." In the case of men like Whitfield and James Brown (whose 1967 smash was "Cold Sweat"), I could recognize their genius and still find them repulsive. As much as I love men, I have no tolerance for men devoid of charm.

My own musical charm, considerable in my own mind and in the minds of my champions like Jim Lewis and Clarence Paul, was not winning me a wide audience. I compared myself with other artists who were selling. I heard Sam & Dave, whom I had met through Marrie Early in Miami, sing "Soul Man" and loved it. I heard Wilson Pickett, who had come up in Detroit, sing "Funky Broadway" and loved it. Sam & Dave and Pickett were working for Wexler. I was working for peanuts. Why? I was certain that I had good taste in music, was in tune with the times, and could sing my ass off, yet I was going nowhere fast.

I was out of town working when Detroit broke out in a riot that same summer. I called home right away to make sure Mama, Sister, and Terrye were okay. They hardly sounded alarmed, but I was a little disappointed that I had missed the excitement. I wanted to see the tanks roving the streets. My own political consciousness was closer to the Panthers than to Martin Luther King, Jr. It took me many years after King's death to realize that his methodology was practically and spiritually more sound than my eye-for-an-eye, tooth-for-a-tooth attitude. At the time, though, I was not impressed with what felt like his submissive approach. I related to warriors, not pacifists. And given my attitude toward the hypocrisy of the church, it didn't help that he was a preacher who had formed his politics from a Christian perspective.

ater that same year, I started working with Grover Washington, Jr. Any sane woman would have to fall in love with Grover. He was going on twenty-four, handsome, immensely talented, good-hearted, and one of the most lyrical saxophonists of his generation. In addition to being a wonderfully kind man, he had an open-hearted approach to music. Unlike a lot of the jazz guys who looked down on R&B, Grover was a musical liberal, not an elitist. He knew it was all good. That's why in the seventies, when other jazz artists were complaining about the crass marketplace, Grover had commercial success. Social snobs are bad, but jazz snobs are even worse. Sweet Grover didn't have a snobbish bone in his body.

We became a couple and went round and round about getting married. He even took me home to meet his parents in Buffalo.

But for all the genuine love between us, we were caught up in romantic dramas outside our relationship. I was still carrying a torch for Clarence Paul and Grover had fallen for a prostitute he'd met in Philly. Distracted by hopeless situations, we thought our affair would help us forget old flames. It didn't. But for a while we did make beautiful music together.

We played Small's, my old stomping grounds in Harlem. Like Jim Lewis, Grover became my teacher. He had me sitting at the piano, learning chords and voicings. He taught me about saxophonists—Dexter Gordon, Stan Getz, Cannonball Adderly, Paul Desmond—the way Jim had taught me about singers. One night King Curtis, one of the great R&B saxophonists, stopped by the club.

"Oh, man," Grover said, "I can't play with that cat in the room."

"You not only can play, baby," I said, "you *will* play. And you *will* play your ass off."

Grover blew beautifully.

"You're so bad you worry me," King said to Grover's face. "But you got no worries yourself. You gonna be bigger than all of us."

In December of 1967, Grover and I were working Newark, New Jersey. He went for a walk while I napped in our hotel room. I woke up in the early evening and saw him sitting in a chair next to the bed with a newspaper in his hand. His eyes said something was wrong.

"What is it?"

"Your friend is dead."

"Which friend?"

"Otis Redding."

"How . . . why . . . what happened?" I was shocked.

"Airplane crash in Wisconsin. Him and some of the Bar-Kays."

"Otis is gone?"

"I'm afraid so."

He was twenty-six, this rolling thunderball of soul. I thought about those times, only a few years back, when he had opened for me with a show ten times more powerful than mine. Then I thought about his climb to the top. That made me happy, not only because he was a good man, but because he proved that our kind of singing has universal appeal. As a vocalist, he never compromised. Compromise raw soul and you wind up with no soul. Otis was all soul. In 1968, a couple of months after his death, you heard "(Sittin' on) The Dock of the Bay" on every radio station and every record player on the planet. He died young, but he died strong. And his music keeps getting stronger.

I met Rudy Robinson playing the clubs in Detroit. His group was called Rudy Robinson and the Hungry Five. Rudy was a bum, a drunk, and a genius. I hated him with all my might and I loved him even more. He was my musical twin. He read my musical mind. He was probably the best keyboardist in the city, Earl Van Dyke included. Like Earl, he could play lightning-fast jazz and molasses-slow blues. He read and wrote music like a professor, and he drank like a fish. He had a huge complex about never being called by Motown. The Motown session players—the Funk Brothers—got all the work and, ultimately, all the major recognition. Rudy lived and died virtually unknown.

He was a regular at D-Town, the anti-Motown label begun by Mike Hanks, a guy who loved going around town saying, "Fuck

Berry Gordy. He was falling off his tricycle when I was buying my second Eldorado." Along with Johnnie Mae Matthews and Robert West, Mike was among the early label pioneers who were overshadowed and outshone by Berry. Hanks never got over it. He bought a little house down the street from Motown on East Grand—Berry was on West Grand—and kept turning out records that got little play. Some say Berry shut him down with the deejays. Who knows? All I know is that Rudy was his main music man and that Rudy, with his major-league talent, always felt stuck in the minors.

Jim had opposed the merger of me and Rudy from the start. Because he didn't know Rudy, he didn't understand the depth of his musicianship. And while Jim was always arguing that I needed a band of my own, he was certain Rudy was the wrong bandleader. Until . . .

One night Rudy came to the musicians' union to pay his overdue dues. Jim and I happened to be there. I seized the opportunity. I said, "Jim, Rudy can play anything."

"Let's go over to the piano and see," Jim challenged.

"Cool," said Rudy.

Rudy calmly sat down at the keyboard, looked at Jim, and said, "Name any tune."

"Let me hear 'Lotus Blossom.'"

"Billy Strayhorn. Ain't nothing by Strayhorn I don't know." And with that, Rudy played the thing like he had written it.

"You got lucky on that one," said Jim. "Give me 'If You Could See Me Now.'"

"Tadd Dameron out of Cleveland," Rudy remembered. "Sarah sang it. Beautiful changes." Next thing we knew, Rudy danced through the changes of that song with such grace that I could swear he wasn't drunk. But he was. And yet the drinking only improved his playing.

After a half-hour, after Woody Herman songs and Dizzy Gillespie songs, Irving Berlin songs and Percy Mayfield songs, Jim conceded. Rudy had played every single one flawlessly.

"You're a brilliant stupid muthafucka," was all Jim could say. "You deserve Bettye and she deserves you. If you two don't wind up killing each other, you'll do fine. Rudy Robinson, you're the best fuckin' piano man in town and, Bettye LaVette, you're the best fuckin' singer even if you are a stubborn bitch."

Having made the final statement of the night, Jim went out like a light. And I had myself the accompanist I'd always dreamed of. So when I heard songs like "What Condition My Condition Is In," I knew that, between me and Rudy, we'd find a way to make it my own.

One night at some local joint, I was singing my set—the usual mix of my singles together with my interpretations of songs by Marvin and Bobby Bland—when Ollie McLaughlin came in. Like Mike Hanks, Ollie was another small-time Detroit label owner. His track record wasn't bad. He had a smash with Barbara Lewis, "Hello Stranger," another with the Capitols, "Cool Jerk," as well as Deon Jackson's "Love Makes the World Go Round." He was no one I could ignore. When he heard my version of "What Condition My Condition Is In," he told me, "Bettye, if you're willing, we're cutting this thing next week."

You know I was willing. I recorded it along with a few other songs—"Almost" and "Get Away"—for his Karen label. "Condition" made some noise in Detroit. Everyone who heard it liked it, but it was strictly local. I was feeling strictly local.

"No need to feel that way," said Ollie. "I'm getting Ahmet

Ertegun to release those Karen singles of yours." Ertegun ran Atlantic.

"And he's heard my stuff?"

"Heard it and loved it."

"And he'll put money behind it?"

"Yes, ma'am. Count on it."

Maybe Ahmet heard those singles, maybe Ahmet loved them, maybe Ahmet even put money behind them. But the result of my second go-round with Atlantic was virtually the same as the first: an initial burst of enthusiasm followed by an alarmingly loud silence.

Back to square one.

Muthafucka.

Changing Conditions

Marvin Gaye was a delicate soul, a soft-spoken man with an easy laugh and a poetic spirit. Later, people said he was a rebel at Motown, but the Marvin I knew was get-along go-along. Clarence Paul, who called him Gates, was always on his case for not being assertive enough.

Marvin's close friends were always concerned about his marriage to Anna Gordy. Along with her sister Gwen, they were the Zsa Zsa and Eva Gabor of Detroit. (I didn't know their younger sister, Loucye, who died young. Sister Esther, who ran Motown's management department, was a straight arrow, although her husband, George Edwards, a Michigan state representative, spent years trying to lure me to bed.) We knew how Anna took advantage of her husband's mild-mannered vulnerability. We all knew of her close relationships with other men, including Aretha's dad, the Reverend C. L. Franklin. We never stopped urging Marvin to beat her ass. But Marvin never would. He knew that injuring the boss's sister would injure his career.

Meanwhile, the people who loved Marvin—everyone in Detroit—kept on him: "Leave the bitch! Beat the bitch! Get the fuck out of that marriage!" So when Clarence called me one day and said, "Gates called and said he threw the bitch's clothes out on the street," I screamed with delight. Marvin, Clarence, and I partied all night. The liberation of Marvin was like the liberation of France. A beautiful spirit was renewed. Shortly thereafter, he started writing *What's Going On*, his gift to the world.

While Marvin started to use his art to express philosophical and theological feelings, I was witness to another major shift in music. It happened only a few blocks from where I lived on Trowbridge—at my old stomping grounds, Phelps Lounge on Oakland. George Clinton, who had once written for Motown, had the Parliaments. "(I Wanna) Testify" was the hit they were promoting during their gig at Phelps. Like all the guy groups at the time, they were dressed in standard show threads—slick silk suits, alligator shoes, processed do's. Funky as the devil, they put on a great show. We were booked for a week solid, but after the first night, something strange happened. George and his boys started dropping acid.

On the first night, before taking LSD, George wore his process in waves. By the second night, he was tripping; he soaked his head under water so that his do became undone. That was nothing compared to night three. Instead of his usual razor-sharp suit, George came out wearing nothing but a diaper held by a big pin!

Everyone in the club screamed. What was this crazy muthafucka doing?

George gave me some acid and decades later I'm still having flashbacks. I never took it again, but George got deeper into it. Just watching him, I could feel myself tripping. Between this gig at Phelps and another ten days at the 20 Grand, I witnessed the birth of psychedelic funk.

Norman Whitfield, that nasty Motown producer, witnessed it as well. He was there every night taking notes. He knew that George was reacting to the crazy changes happening in the youth culture—the explosion caused by the hippies who said, as far as style goes, that the sky was the limit. If Jimi Hendrix could kiss the sky and burn up his guitar onstage, George wasn't going to be left behind. George had the foresight and guts to take it to the next level. Funk didn't have to be restricted to the past. Funk could be the future. So he had his band put on futuristic outfits, and under a banner of different names—Parliament, Funkadelic, P-Funk—Clinton blazed a new trail in Detroit at about the same time Sly and the Family Stone were carrying on in California.

Following George's lead, Whitfield went to the studio and came out with his psychedelic productions for the Temptations with Dennis Edwards, who'd been singing around town for years, replacing David Ruffin. Whitfield managed to follow Sly and Clinton into the Age of Aquarius with his big hits for the Temps like "Cloud Nine," "I Can't Get Next to You," and "Ball of Confusion."

While Clinton and Whitfield were listening to Sly Stone, I was listening to Kenny Rogers and the First Edition. I liked my version of "What Condition My Condition Is In," but Jim Lewis didn't. He never liked any of my records. He didn't think they did me justice. But when he learned that Kenny Rogers was coming to the 20 Grand, he was sharp enough to urge me to meet him and play him my interpretation of his hit.

"And what am I supposed to do—slip backstage and give him my record?" I asked Jim.

"Exactly."

"Why don't you do that?"

"Because you have a better-looking booty than I do."

"It's not my style to chase down some singer and beg him to listen to my record."

"I'll take you over there. I'll hold your hand."

Jim accompanied me to Kenny's dressing room. It was a good meeting. Kenny had great smoke and a portable record player. He put on my version of his song, closing his eyes as he listened. I didn't know what the hell he was thinking.

"Goddamn!" he said, when the record had played.

"Goddamn good or goddamn bad?" I asked.

"Goddamn *great*! I like your version better than ours."

"You do?"

"Do you have a deal?"

"No."

"Well, I'm calling my brother right now. He's down in Nashville starting a new label."

Kenny picked up the phone and dialed.

"Hey, Lelan, have you heard of a singer called Bettye LaVette?"

I didn't know what was being said on the other end of the line. I only heard Kenny say, "Wow! That's amazing!"

"What's he saying?" I asked.

"He's saying he was the national promo director on your 'Let

Me Down Easy.' Not only has he heard of you, he's crazy about you. He wants to cut a record right away. Talk to him."

Lelan Rogers was excited. He had just named his new label Silver Fox after his silver mane. His financial backer was Shelby Singleton whose Plantation Records was riding high after selling six million copies of Jeannie C. Riley's "Harper Valley P.T.A." Singleton had also bought out Sam Phillips's Sun Records, Elvis's original label, along with Sam's entire catalogue.

"Shelby has money to burn," said Lelan. "He trusts my instincts and my instincts tell me that you're the next Aretha."

"Keep talking, Lelan," I said. "That's music to my ears."

"The way Wexler took Aretha to Muscle Shoals, I'm taking you to Memphis. You heard of Jim Dickinson? He got him a rhythm section down there with Charlie Freeman on guitar that's on fire. They're gonna burn you up."

"Burn, baby, burn," was all I could say.

Sounds of Memphis, the studio where we worked, had a different vibe than studios in Detroit and New York. Punctuality was not a priority. Neither was preparation. In Detroit and New York, most of the session players were accomplished jazz musicians who read and wrote music. They were precise and accustomed to working on a schedule. Detroit was an assembly-line city. Products kept moving. New York was a time-is-money city. No fooling around in the studio. Memphis was all about fooling around.

Not to criticize, because the fooling around was fun. The fooling around created some sweet funk. Wexler understood that when he stole the Muscle Shoals rhythm section for Aretha from Rick Hall's FAME label and brought them to Atlantic. Later, he'd do the same thing with these boys I started working with—Jim, Charlie, Tommy McClure on bass, Sammy Creason on drums, and Michael Utley on organ. After Wexler landed in Miami, he recruited Dickinson's band to Criterion Studios. They renamed themselves the Dixie Flyers and eventually became Kris Kristofferson's band. When I knew them, they had no name and no money. Same thing for the horn players on my Memphis sessions—Wayne Jackson, Floyd Newman, Andrew Love, and Ed Logan. They got famous later as the Memphis Horns, but during our time together recording for Lelan, they were as broke as I was.

It didn't take long to get used to that slow Tennessee trot that marked the rhythm of recording in Memphis. Musical arrangements were made up on the spot. Sessions started an hour or two or three behind schedule. No one was in a hurry and no one seemed uptight. Shelby Singleton had sprung for a big budget and that meant extra money for recreational purposes. These white boys liked popping the speed pills used by truck drivers. Weed was plentiful.

Wayne Jackson, the trumpet player, and I took a liking to each other. He was a married man who didn't act like one. I fell in love with Wayne, a good guy, a down-home hippie. The song he wrote that I recorded in Memphis says it all—"At the Mercy of a Man." Soon he was camping out in my hotel room. Sometimes he'd get up early in the morning, run out to the airstrip, jump in the little plane he piloted, and buzz the hotel. A few hours later, he was back in my bed.

I could deal with this new way of making music—hanging with the guys, staying stoned, getting to the studio when it felt right, recording with no preset plan, going with the flow. All the elements seemed right to catapult me to the next level. This was the heartland of southern soul, where whites and blacks were combining forces to create smashes for Wilson Pickett, Etta James, and Clarence Carter. I was in the thick of the Nashville/Memphis/Muscle Shoals/muddy-Mississippi hit-making territory. With my voice and the right song, there was no reason I couldn't sing my way back into the big time.

We were all convinced we'd found the right song—"He Made a Woman Outta Me," a rough-and-tough anthem about a girl "born on a levee, a little bit south of Montgomery." At sixteen, Joe Henry comes up the river and makes a woman of the girl. I related. It was an unapologetic, no-holds-barred story of a sweet deflowering. The horn punches were bright and clean, the lead vocal was convincing, and Lelan Rogers deemed it a hit.

It reached number 25 on the R&B chart and looked like it would cross over to the pop side, when someone said they'd heard the song on white radio sung by someone else.

"Who?" I asked.

"Bobbie Gentry."

Two years earlier, Gentry had a smash with "Ode to Billie Joe." When I heard her version of "He Made a Woman Outta Me," though, I knew I had outsung her. I knew I had a hit. But then radio stations started banning my version because of a semi-sexy line in the song. They took that line out of Gentry's version so hers got played. She got the hit. I'm still mad. Years later, when I was asked to sing on a Bobbie Gentry tribute album, I said, "Hell, no."

Muthafucka.

But Lelan was determined to get me over. He didn't give up.

He found a song he was certain would work—"Do Your Duty." Not only was the do-it-to-me message raucous and right, the tune was by Ronnie Shannon, the man who wrote Aretha's breakthrough "I Never Loved a Man (The Way I Love You)."

Unfortunately, "Do Your Duty" did nothing.

"Well," said Lelan, "if Wexler can make money getting Aretha to sing Willie Nelson's 'Night Life,' I think you can sell the hell out of Joe South's 'Games People Play.' What do you say?"

What was I supposed to say? I said yes. I'd try anything. Besides, I liked the song. I don't know why the record didn't sell, but it didn't. That didn't stop Lelan, though. He wasn't out of ideas.

"Just signed Hank Ballard. You know Hank, don't you?" he asked.

"Sure, I know Hank. Mama and them danced to 'Work with Me, Annie.' He did the original 'Twist.'"

"Remember when him and the Midnighters had 'Let's Go, Let's Go, Let's Go'?"

"I was a little girl, but I remember."

"Well, he wants to re-record it as a duet with you."

I was happy to work with Hank. In the studio, though, his memory started to fade. I had to both sing my part and whisper the lyrics in Hank's ear. The same thing was true when we did "Hello Sunshine," a song that both Wilson Pickett and Aretha had recorded.

Lelan loved everything I did. He was going to put out a series of singles, including my version of "Take Another Little Piece of My Heart." Moneyman Shelby Singleton had bought "Let Me Down Easy" from Calla and was going to group it with these recent recordings in what would be my first album.

But then came my buzzard luck. Shelby and Lelan fell out of love. I never learned the details, but the details didn't matter. Suddenly Lelan's label went down the toilet along with all the songs I'd done in Memphis. The idea of a full-tilt R&B album never happened. In 1969 and 1970, these little singles came dribbling out of a faucet that soon went dry. Lelan disappeared, and another set of grandiose schemes, in which I would take my rightful place in the Golden Age of Soul, went for naught.

But I was too foolish to fall into despair. I knew something good was gonna happen someday. And I'd be damned if that day wasn't coming soon.

Child of the Seventies

That day came sooner rather than later. Local label man and Ahmet Ertegun's running buddy Ollie McLaughlin never gave up on me. Ollie took me into the studio to cut Neil Young's "Heart of Gold." Rudy Robinson wrote an arrangement that scared me to death—that's how good it was.

"Bettye," said Ollie, in his slight English accent. "This is the one. This is the one that's sending you over the top."

"Glad to hear that, Ollie, but all these singles are wearing me out. I want an album. I need an album."

This was, after all, the era when FM radio was playing whole albums. Aretha Franklin had nearly a dozen albums on Columbia and, in just four years, eight on Atlantic. I had none. The music-loving public was eating up albums. Marvin Gaye's *What's Going On* was called the best album of all time. Some of my best friends in the business, the O'Jays, were putting out albums with Gamble and Huff in Philly. Where were *my* albums? How was it possible, with all the singles I had cut and all the promises made, that I didn't have a single 33⅓ LP with my picture plastered on the cover?

"It'll come," said Ollie. "I'm going to play this 'Heart of Gold' for Ahmet. When he hears it, he'll let you make an album."

"I've heard that before."

"Ahmet loved the earlier stuff you did with me. I can promise you that he's going to love this even more."

"If he does, it'll be my third go-around with Atlantic. I feel like I'm on the Atlantic merry-go-round."

"But this time you're gonna grab that brass ring."

"I want the gold ring," I said.

"'Heart of Gold' is the ticket, baby. You wait and see."

I didn't have to wait long.

"You sitting down, Bettye?" asked Ollie over the phone.

"Is the news that bad?" I asked.

"It's that good. Ahmet heard 'Heart of Gold.' He flipped the fuck out. He's sending you to Muscle Shoals."

"With Wexler?"

"Wexler's in Florida. He doesn't go to Muscle Shoals no more. The boy who's tearing it up in Muscle Shoals is Brad Shapiro."

"The guy who just did 'Don't Knock My Love' for Wilson Pickett?"

"That's right. Went number one. Shapiro's hot as a fire-cracker."

"So you're talking about an album, not just a bunch of singles?"

"Shapiro's talking about twelve songs, a whole concept, wall-to-wall hits. They're using the same musicians, same arrangers, and same studio where they cut Pickett's hits."

"I'm gonna repeat my question, Ollie, 'cause this time I want to make sure I'm not dreaming. I want to make sure the shit is clear. We're talking an album, not just singles."

"Bettye, your first album, your debut Atlantic album, is not only as good as done, it's as good as gold."

In the winter of 1972, I flew to Muscle Shoals and met Brad Shapiro.

"You ready to sing?" he asked.

"You ready with the songs?"

"Here they are. Listen to them and see if you like 'em."

I loved them. Brad had written three originals—"Fortune Teller," "Soul Tambourine," and "Our Own Love Song." Some of the other tunes had a country feel in the style of Percy Sledge's "When a Man Loves a Woman." There was also a poignant message song, "All the Black and White Children."

The one that really slew me, though, was Joe Simon's "Your Time to Cry." I put on a new title and sang it as "Your Turn to Cry." I'm a harsh critic of my own stuff. I know when my voice is off and my performance lame. I don't think every performance of mine is brilliant or every recording of mine a masterpiece. But I knew goddamn well that "Your Turn to Cry" was as good as anything out there. In every fiber of my being, I knew it was a hit.

After the vocal was cut in Muscle Shoals, the horns added in

Memphis, and the strings overdubbed in Miami, the album was ready to go.

Back in Detroit, I played the pre-release tapes for my friends. Mama and Sister went crazy for it. Cousin Margaret broke out into a big smile and said, "The long wait is over, Betty Jo." Even the critic of critics, Professor Jim Lewis, said, "Shapiro definitely brought out the best in you. This is first-rate. I'm proud of you."

I was proud of myself. Now it was just a question of waiting for the icing on the cake—the photography session for the cover, the packaging, and the promotional tour.

Jerry Greenberg had taken over from the semi-retired Jerry Wexler and was running the day-to-day operations at Atlantic under Ahmet Ertegun. Because I knew Ollie had spoken to Ahmet and Ahmet told him the album was great, I was convinced it couldn't miss. When the first single dropped, Clarence Paul said, "You're calling it 'Your Turn to Cry,' but I'm saying it's your turn to hit the charts."

There was talk of a big tour. Someone in the Atlantic PR department sent me tickets to fly all over the country to promote the single and follow-up album. When someone suggested calling it *Child of the Seventies*, I said, "Hell, yes." The sixties had not been kind to me. The seventies were my decade.

I was getting ready for the tour when the phone rang.

"Bettye?"

"Yes."

"I'm calling from Atlantic."

"How's the single selling?"

"Fine."

"I got those tickets for the big promo tour. Your PR department has been great. I'm eager to get out and do my thing."

"That's why I'm calling."

I didn't like the tone of his voice.

"What's wrong?"

"We've decided not to go forth with the project. Please return the plane tickets."

There was nothing to do but crawl under the dining room table, assume the fetal position, and not move for two weeks. I was completely and absolutely devastated.

Buzzard luck.

Muthafucka.

I have to call it something more than the blues. The blues will come late at night or early in the morning, stay an hour or two, and be gone. The blues will darken your day or ruin your evening, but a stiff drink or a potent joint can usually chase the blues away. Depression is something else.

Curled up under that dining room table, I didn't wanna go anywhere. I didn't wanna talk to anyone, didn't wanna see anyone, didn't wanna move. I wanted the floor to open up and swallow me whole. Nothing Mama or Sister said mattered. I liked seeing Terrye. She was twelve years old and on the verge of becoming a beautiful teenager. But even the presence of my only child didn't pull me from the depths of despair.

They say hope is helpful, but expectations will get you in trouble. Hope means you think there's a chance that things will come out right. An expectation means you damn well demand it. After all this time, I did expect to have an album out. Promises were made at Atlantic by everyone from the janitor to the president. My producer, who had fed the industry a slew of hits, told me that

Child of the Seventies was the highlight of his career. "There are at least four singles on this record that can go top ten," Brad Shapiro said. These were statements that wouldn't stop whirling around my head as I hid from the world, not answering calls, not venturing out, not even wanting to look out the window.

It took the Professor to break the depression.

One day Jim Lewis just showed up. I didn't even want to open the door.

"Give me a cup of coffee," he said.

"Go out and buy your own damn cup of coffee."

"Nice to know I'm welcome here."

"It's not you, Jim. You know that. This time it's not all that easy getting going again."

"I understand."

"If you understand, why are you over here bothering me?"

"'Cause I got a gig for you."

"Phelps?"

"Something better. A jingle."

"How much does it pay?"

"Nothing right now."

"So that's the good news? A job that pays nothing."

"It's a talent contest. Schaefer Beer. If you sing their jingle and win, you get good money. Plays all over the country."

"So it's amateur hour."

"No, Bettye LaVette, it isn't amateur hour. Other professional singers are entering. The money is serious. And there are different versions. You do a funk version, another with a big band, a ballad version—you get the idea."

"I don't like the idea."

"Why?"

"Because it's a horse race. I have too many damn records out there for me to do something for free."

"You're telling me you don't need the money."

"You know goddamn well I need the money."

"Then swallow your pride, girl, and be grateful I'm bringing this to you."

"You get on my nerves, Jim Lewis, you really do."

A week later I was in the studio singing the jingle. A few weeks after that I learned I had won the contest and Schaefer Beer was using my version coast to coast. "Schaefer is the one beer to have when you're having more than one." These days that ad wouldn't be politically correct. You're only supposed to have one. Back in the seventies, you could have as many as you wanted— and the ads told you so. Maybe I won because that was my attitude. I sang with conviction. I was representing the true feelings of us "real" drinkers. Once again, Jim had come through.

The early seventies weren't a tough time for just me. It was a tough time for my hometown too. Berry Gordy and his gang had picked up—lock, stock, and barrel—and moved the Motown office to L.A. In the sixties, Detroit was at the center of the musical universe. In the seventies, Detroit was flat-out abandoned. Of the Gordy family, only Esther, who had a great sense of civic responsibility, stayed around to represent the company. But that really meant nothing. Motown's greatest resources—its stars, studios, marketing and promotional teams—were all in Hollywood.

Baseball fans say that when the Dodgers left Brooklyn,

Brooklyn was never the same. That was equally true of Motown and Detroit. Because of our capacity to design and manufacture cars, we were once the pride of America. With the advent of modern soul music, we revitalized that pride in an artistic context. When that context was removed, dreams were dashed. In short, Berry was saying, *Fuck Detroit, the real gold's in L.A.* Even the artists most reluctant to leave—like Marvin Gaye—finally caved in and followed the boss.

The last major thing Marvin recorded in Detroit was *What's Going On.* If you listen to that record, it's very Detroit in its description of a soldier coming back to America after being traumatized in Vietnam. When Marvin asks "What's going on?" he's asking what's going on in Detroit, not Hollywood. And when he sings about "Inner City Blues," those blues are coming out of the streets of Detroit, not L.A.

The post-Motown era in Detroit wasn't pretty. The big stars were gone. The big clubs were empty. The big money had vanished. As one who was left behind, I can't be too sanctimonious, because if I had made it in New York, I would have stayed in New York. Every time I came home—and I came home dozens of times—it was because I had to. At the same time, I was just a solo singer. I hadn't impacted my city the way Berry had. He'd created an empire. He was an economic force to be reckoned with, and when the force was no longer there, all of us felt the loss. Detroit got a permanent case of the blues.

This was the mood of the city when I was booked at Phelps on the same bill as the great Jackie Wilson. After "Higher and Higher," Jackie Wilson began a descent that had him falling lower and lower. If you were a true Jackie Wilson fan, though, you'd always rank him on top. And I was among the truest of all Jackie fans. He was more than just the most flamboyant singer to ever come out of Detroit. The man was mega-sexy. It wasn't that he was all that good-looking—Clarence Paul was far more handsome—but he was a pure expression of sexual energy. Something about his mouth made women melt. He had a smile, a swagger, a body language that spoke volumes. In the early days, even before he became a big star, he had a bevy of women. When he did become a star, the bevy turned into an army.

When Mr. Phelps told me I was on the same bill as Jackie, I was excited. When I met him at the club, he kissed me, just as he kissed all his female fans. I immediately became one of his groupies. I was intent on having this man, if only for one night.

The engagement was for a week. The first few nights were cool. He wasn't the Jackie Wilson of five or six years earlier. Time had taken its toll. His dance moves had been modified and his voice had weakened. His hard times were showing. But he could still sing. He was also generous in complimenting my singing. By the end of the week, we were buddies, and after the Saturday night show, I took him home to my blue basement. Exhausted, he stretched out on the couch and closed his eyes.

I had to run upstairs and tell Mama and Sister the news. And naturally they had to come down and meet him. It was a thrilling moment for all concerned. And even though all the cocaine we blew diminished Jackie's sexual drive—it was mainly a matter of hugging and kissing—I was nonetheless honored to be in his arms. When I awoke the next morning, I looked over and saw Jackie Wilson sleeping in my bed. Happiness was mine.

. . .

W hat do you mean you slept with Jackie Wilson?" asked Clarence, who was calling from L.A. No longer with Motown, he was doing freelance music hustles in Hollywood.

"You know how they have those signs on some houses in New England that say 'George Washington Slept Here,' well, I'm putting up a sign outside my house that says 'Jackie Wilson Slept Here.'"

"Was he good?" asked Clarence.

"He was tired."

"And how about you, aren't you tired of Detroit?"

"I do admit the city feels a little lonely."

"Come out here. I'll send you a ticket."

"What am I going to do out there?"

"That producer who did your last record is out here."

"Brad Shapiro?"

"That's the one. Maybe he can still help you."

"Atlantic in New York shut me down."

"I know. But Atlantic in L.A. has its own money to spend. Besides, how cold is it today in Detroit?"

"Fifteen."

"How does seventy-five degrees sound to you?"

"When did you say you're sending that ticket?"

The Institute for
Sexual Intercourse

At the start of the seventies in L.A., land of eternal sunshine, I was looking to get out of the dark. After Atlantic dumped me, I had enough depression to last a lifetime. Despair was not my friend, and now I was about to see whether Brad Shapiro was. Brad tried. He turned me on to some of the Atlantic folks in L.A., who found a little money for me to go into the studio with Clarence. This time I wrote two songs that described my situation with perfect accuracy—"Waiting for Tomorrow" and "Livin' Life on a Shoestring." Leslie Drayton wrote the charts. Because Clarence was close to Ike Turner, we recorded at Ike's Bolic Sounds studio, where Ike and Tina cut most of their material. That's where I met Johnny "Guitar" Watson, the original "Gangster of Love." Like Ike, Johnny was one of the major architects of the tight funk that groups like the Ohio Players and

Rufus were building careers on. Also like Ike, Johnny could snort up more blow than a brand-new Hoover.

I've been told that the songs I did at Bolic have a definite sound—the highly orchestrated "Curtis Mayfield meets Isaac Hayes meets Marvin Gaye" early-seventies feel. I wasn't thinking that way. I was just singing my heart out. I was singing, "A wing and a prayer is all I got to lean on." I was singing for my supper, for this new group of Atlantic execs who might finally put out something people would buy.

We had a blast in the studio. The blow was plentiful. The compliments were generous. Clarence loved it. Ike loved it. Tina loved it. The Atlantic people said they liked it and would get back to me.

"While we're waiting," said Clarence, "let's catch up with Marvin. Him and Ed Townsend are in the Motown studio up in Hollywood."

Since he put out *What's Going On*, Marvin had done an edgy sound track for the movie *Trouble Man*. It was a slyly autobiographical, mainly instrumental suite of songs. Now everyone was waiting to see what he'd do next.

Like Clarence, Ed Townsend was a veteran singer/songwriter from the fifties. His big hit was "For Your Love." He and Marvin were in great spirits when we arrived. It was a wonderful reunion. Ed had introduced Marvin to a sixteen-year-old girl, Janis Hunter, who had rocked his world. He was crazy in love. He had only one thought in his head and, together with Ed, was able to express it in a song that said it all: "Let's Get It On."

"What do you think?" he asked Clarence, after playing us the track.

"You're the only guy I know who can go from 'What's Going On' to 'Let's Get It On,'" said Clarence.

"Is that good or bad?" asked Marvin.

"Don't matter none," said Clarence. "'Cause whatever it is, it's a stone smash."

Marvin asked all of us—Clarence and me included—to help on backgrounds. Before that happened, Marvin talked about Jan for an hour. Then he and Clarence played poker for another hour, arguing and joking back and forth, all the while smoking joints and blowing cocaine. When it was finally time to record the backgrounds, everyone did something. That was always the case when Marvin made music. He had his friends help out—whether patting our feet, snapping our fingers, or, in this case, clapping our hands. We had a large time.

We were all hoping that Marvin's new love, even though she was seventeen years younger than he was, would make him happy. His ex-wife, who was seventeen years older than Marvin, certainly had not. Whatever craziness Marvin might be going through made him even more lovable to his closest friends. His mentors—Clarence Paul, Ed Townsend, and Harvey Fuqua— thought Marvin could do no wrong. For ladies like me, Marvin's charm was singular. The irony was that he wasn't the macho man he wanted to be, and yet that gentleness—that extreme vulnerability—is what women loved.

In contrast, Mac Rebennack, known to all as Dr. John, hardly seemed vulnerable at all. That's not to say he didn't have his own flavor of funk and homegrown charm. Allen Toussaint had used the Meters in cutting Dr. John's Atlantic album *In the Right Place*, which included his big hit, "Right Place Wrong Time." I liked the record but wasn't sure why Atlantic was pushing his while mine was still in cold storage. Anyway, Dr. John and I bonded over our love of weed and straight-up R&B. I needed work and he hired me to sing background on his *Right Place* tour. During rehearsal, I couldn't help but sing little fills in my parts. I thought they were tasty and added to the overall vocal vibe. Dr. John didn't agree.

"Can you sing it straight, Bettye?" he said.

"Probably not."

"Can you try?"

I tried, failed, and got fired. Dr. John gave me some money anyway—and an ounce of pot. For years I maintained that my greatest claim to fame was being fired by Dr. John. When I saw him recently, he said, "Baby, you gotta stop telling people that I fired you. I'd never fire a singer as good as you."

"Well, you did," I said. "But I love you anyway."

We hugged and renewed our friendship, and it's still going strong.

Back in the early seventies, I was still dead broke. I had started my L.A. journey in Hollywood, and as my money ran out, I found myself down-and-out in Watts. Something had to happen fast. Maybe Atlantic would like those Clarence Paul–produced songs and release them. Maybe Atlantic would finally give me some real money.

Wishful thinking. "Waiting for Tomorrow" and "Livin' Life on a Shoestring" were the real-life truths about my situation, but Atlantic didn't feel it. They weren't about to release my stuff.

I finally got an honest answer from one of their L.A. execs. "Look, Bettye," he said. "Wexler is long gone and Ahmet is busy signing white rock and rollers. Jerry Greenberg isn't inclined to champion you, and Brad Shapiro is getting ready to work with Millie Jackson in Muscle Shoals."

"Why does he think Millie Jackson can have Muscle Shoals hits and I can't?" I asked.

"Brad's not the problem. Atlantic is. Forget Atlantic. If you need some quick money, I know a place where you can get it."

"Where?"

"Well, it's kind of a sex clinic."

"A sex clinic? What the hell is that? A fancy name for a whorehouse? I'm not turning tricks."

"It's not a whorehouse and you won't be turning tricks. A lot of actresses and singers work over there. Just go by and see what they have to say."

When your money is funny, you do funny things. When I was twenty-seven, my money was very funny. That's why I went to this building on Santa Monica Boulevard, right next door to the Pussycat Theater, where the recently released *Deep Throat* was playing. I looked at the directory in the building lobby and there it was, in plain language, INSTITUTE FOR SEXUAL INTERCOURSE, located on the second floor, Unit B. I sighed and walked up the stairs, opened the door and introduced myself to a lady sitting behind a receptionist's desk.

"I'm here to see about work," I said, swallowing all pride.

"Have you been recommended?"

"I have." I gave the name of the man who told me about the place.

"Have a seat. Our director will see you in a moment."

The director was a middle-aged man with six chins. He sat in an office overlooking the marquee for *Deep Throat*.

"This is a reputable clinic," he said. "We're here to help men with sexual problems."

"How does that work?" I asked.

"They come for instruction."

"And not to get laid?"

"No, not at all. You are never completely nude."

"Only half nude?"

"You wear a bikini."

"And what does the john wear?"

"He isn't a john, he's a legitimate client."

"What does the legitimate client wear?"

"His underwear."

"So I'm in a bikini, he's in his drawers, and then what happens?"

"You show him what positions are most suitable for sex."

"You're kidding."

"I'm not. Many men have no idea about what positions to take."

"You mean to tell me men don't know they go on top and we go on the bottom?"

"Maybe they know that, but maybe they don't know it can work the other way."

"It doesn't take a lot of imagination to figure that out."

"Not all men have a lot of imagination."

"Can I be honest?" I asked.

"Of course."

"I'm supposed to teach these men about fucking by pretending to fuck. Is that it?"

"So to speak."

"So it's about dry fucking. It's about humping. They're bouncing on me with their shorts on and come all over themselves."

"Different men have different experiences. Some do ejaculate, but others can't even achieve erections."

"And I'm playing the part of Dr. Feelgood."

"Can you do it?"

"Mister," I said. "I've done a lot worse."

"Fine. Your first client is scheduled for tomorrow afternoon."

My first client wore boxers with bunnies all over them. He was a shy guy who just wanted to get on top of a woman. He didn't even want to bounce, just feel some flesh.

Other clients were far more aggressive. They thought they were paying to actually fuck me. I set them straight in a hurry. If they didn't get the idea, we had a big bouncer outside the door who'd come in and knock them on the head. The bouncer made me feel secure.

I worked four, five days a week. I got used to it. The lack of penetration made all the difference in the world. A lot of these guys were afraid of penetration. They just wanted to bounce up and down a few times, come, and get the hell out. It was easy money.

Then one day we got raided. I didn't understand what for until the owner said that some of his girls turned out to be working women using the institute as a place to fuck their johns. It turned out that at the Institute for Sexual Intercourse there was plenty of penetration—which was when I decided to get out. After a month and two separate police raids, enough was enough.

Solomon Burke is one of my all-time favorite singers. When someone asked Jerry Wexler who was the best soul singer, he said, "Solomon Burke with a borrowed rhythm section." Wexler wasn't wrong. So when the phone rang in my down-and-out Watts flat and the man said he was Solomon Burke, I couldn't have been happier.

"I know who you are, Bettye LaVette," he said. "I like the way you sing, and I want you to open my show."

"I want to sing with you, Solomon Burke," I said. "I'd *love* to sing with you."

"When can you be ready to rehearse?"

"In about an hour."

He laughed and that was it. Two weeks later I was onstage with Solomon Burke in San Francisco.

It had been ten years or so since Solomon had gone to Atlantic and saved the label after Ray Charles had gone over to ABC. Like a lot of singers who had at least one strong string of hits, Solomon's popularity with his core black audience was solid, and whether he was on the charts or not, he could always work. He'd gone from big auditoriums to small clubs, but small clubs were okay with me, especially one called Small's Paradise in Harlem.

"Ever hear of it, Bettye?" Solomon asked.

"Daddy," I said, "I played that club for years. It was my home base."

Solomon loved to be called Daddy. He had dozens of women and hundreds of children. He liked to call me into the bathroom when he was sitting in the tub, naked as a beached whale and nearly as big.

"Bettye," he said, "I still haven't gotten you in my church."

Solomon was a preacher with a mail-order divinity degree. In church, he sat on a throne and wore a crown on his head.

"And you won't be getting me in that church anytime soon," I said.

"You don't think it's good to praise and worship God?"

"If this God of yours is so perfect, I'm wondering why he needs all this praise and worship. Is he that insecure?"

"He's not insecure. We are. We need the security we get when we tell him he's worthy."

"So that's the deal—kiss God's ass and God makes you feel okay."

"You twisting it around."

"You're the one who's twisting to make sense out of something that's plain nonsense."

"How can you live without faith?"

"You need faith, I agree. But faith in what? Faith in the fairy tales you read about in the Bible? I don't think so, Solomon. Faith in other people, faith in yourself."

"But what about faith in a spirit you can't see?"

"If I can't see it, what's the point?"

"Salvation."

"Oh, Lord, save me from this preacher man!"

Solomon laughed and got out of the tub. I liked our conversation, not because I was about to convert to whatever form of Christianity he was peddling, but because he was a genuinely nice guy.

"How you make love to someone that big?" my cousin Margaret asked me.

"Simple," I said. "You sit on him."

When we got to New York, Solomon was surprised to learn that I had my own cadre of fans at Small's. Besides the fans, there were also former boyfriends eager to reignite the flames.

After our last show on our last night, I quietly took one of those boyfriends back to my hotel room. I didn't want to aggravate Solomon, but at the same time I was still singing that song that said, "Ain't nobody's business if I do." We had closed the door behind us and started the first phase of the game of love when we heard Solomon banging on the door.

"You in there, Bettye LaVette?"

I didn't say anything. We waited until we heard his heavy footsteps moving away from the room. Then we got the game going real good.

Next morning when I went down to breakfast, the man in the hotel coffee shop asked, "Aren't you with the Solomon Burke group anymore?"

"I sure am. What do you mean?"

"They left out of here an hour ago for the airport."

I came to find out that Solomon alerted everyone but me that they were flying to Chicago a day early. When I finally contacted the tour manager and asked about my plane ticket, he said, "Solomon told me to cash it in."

"What about paying me my four hundred dollars for this gig in New York?"

"You'll have to talk to Solomon about it."

Flash forward a few decades.

Solomon and I shared the bill for a show in Norway. I was singing "Your Turn to Cry." While I was performing, Solomon sent his son onstage to put a hundred-dollar bill in my hand.

When Solomon died shortly after that, I was certain he did so to avoid paying me the three hundred dollars he still owed me.

Before My Sugar
Turned to Shit

In the mid-seventies, the world wasn't cooperating with me one goddamn bit. In thirteen years, I'd recorded some sixty songs. That's enough for six albums. And yet I still didn't have a single one. I'd been through more labels than I wanted to remember. Even had a small one of my own with Jim called TCA (Twentieth Century Attractions) that didn't go anywhere. In my hometown of Detroit where Motown had exploded in the sixties, Al Green was forging his sound and exploding on the R&B and pop charts. It was water, water, everywhere, but not a drop to drink.

There were singers like Ortheia Barnes who, because she never left Detroit, established a beachhead and played lucrative gigs. But because I was out there chasing rainbows in New York and L.A., I was gone too much of the time to solidify a local base.

After the episode with Solomon Burke in New York, I dragged my broke ass back home. I could always count on the love of

Mama, Sister, Terrye, cousin Margaret, and Jim Lewis. That was comfort, but that wasn't enough. Despite my defeats, my ambition had not died. Neither had my need to pick up where I'd left off with the party people.

Nate's Place, run by a friend of Clarence Paul's, was always good for a party. It was an after-hours joint where you could eat, gamble, and buy cocaine. Something like a speakeasy from an earlier era, Nate's was situated in a house. You had to knock on the front door and be given the nod of approval before gaining admission.

As I walked up the steps of the front porch, two men approached me from the lawn below.

"Who you looking for?" one of them asked.

"Nate," I said. "Tell him Bettye LaVette is here."

"You have to go around the side to get in," said the other.

"No, you don't. I know the drill. Just tell Nate to let me in."

"Jump off the porch," said the bigger one, as he pulled out a gun and aimed it at my head.

I was scared but not completely intimidated. "I'm not jumping off no goddamn porch," I said. "If you want me down, you're gonna have to help me down."

He did just that, reaching out his arm and dragging me off the porch. As he did it, I dropped my diamond watch into the leaves. I was also trying to think of a way to dump the little mink jacket I was wearing over my shoulders, but that wasn't possible. With a gun in my back, they had me walk around the side of the house where they told me to put my hands up in the air.

"What is this shit?" I asked. "Some kind of TV show? Do y'all really know what you're doing?"

"Shut the fuck up, bitch."

"I'm not the kind of woman who shuts up easily. I'm a singer. Singers tend to run off at the mouth."

"What kind of singer?"

"Rhythm-and-blues singer. And if singing hadn't saved me, I'd probably be doing the same as you. I was raised up with the baddest gangstas in Detroit."

"Which ones?" they asked.

I named names: Adolph Ellington, Jimmy Jones, Louisiana Red. These guys were notorious, and my assailants were impressed.

"Sister," they said, "you so cool, why don't you come with us?"

"I'd love to, fellas, but I gotta see my friends inside."

By then some people were leaving and heard us talking. The guys got nervous and ran off—but not before snatching the mink jacket off my shoulders. Nate ran out to see what had happened. I told him and the others I'd been robbed. I should not have mentioned that I dropped my diamond watch in the grass because the people helping me search must have found it—and never said a word.

Muthafuckas.

When Berry Gordy made so much money packaging black music for white people, the majors tried to follow his lead. Marketing consultants were hired to figure out the method. Columbia Records invested heavily in this area. That's why they partnered with Kenneth Gamble and Leon Huff in Philly International Records. Gamble and Huff were the first to produce the Jacksons after they left Motown. Columbia wasn't about to make the same mistake they made with Aretha. They had made major money with Sly and the Family Stone; in the mid-seventies their shining star was Earth, Wind & Fire, whose crossover funk was all the rage. The company had cash to burn.

Through our friendship with Detroit writer Ron Dunbar, Jim and I hooked up with Epic, a Columbia subsidiary. Here we go again.

Was I skeptical? Not really. I couldn't afford to be. I had to believe that this was the break I'd been waiting for. If I didn't buy that line, I'd turn cynical. A cynical attitude would show up in my music. I had to get all excited again and figure that, as I approached thirty, I would finally taste that sweet wine.

I recorded four songs—a cover of Charlie Rich's hit "Behind Closed Doors," "Thank You for Loving Me," "You Made a Believer Out of Me," and the one that expressed my attitude about music execs—"You're a Man of Words, I'm a Woman of Action."

It was great to see my name on a major label. The Epic promo people did get me a few appearances in Chicago.

I was in the Windy City when I called Marrie Early in Miami.

"Hi, Bettye. How you doing, baby?"

"Getting by, Marrie."

"You in Detroit?"

"Chicago."

"Promoting your new record?"

"Yes."

"I love 'You Made a Believer Out of Me.' I think it's going to be a big hit. They're playing it in Miami. I'm playing it every day."

"You're sweet, Marrie, and I love your support, I really do, but I don't think Epic is really behind me. Nothing's really happening sales-wise."

"How 'bout love-wise, Bettye?"

"I had a little dalliance with Pervis Staples when I got here."

"Mavis's brother?"

"The same."

"How was that?"

"Made me miss an interview the next morning. First time that's ever happened."

"It was that good?"

"I'm not saying that. I'm just saying I overslept."

"You seen Gene Chandler?"

"No, you think I should?"

"He's Mr. Chicago, isn't he? I know how he's been hitting on you for years. I also know he's a good businessman. He's got his own label."

"To be honest, Marrie, I never liked him."

"Maybe you could learn to like him. Anyway, if you bump into him, I wouldn't run away. Say hello for me."

Marrie's easygoing attitude about men—and what they could do for you—continued to amaze me. Marrie was so relaxed when it came to the opposite sex. She accepted them the way they were. I saw her avoid their nasty traits while bringing out their goodness. I marveled at how her sunny disposition let her walk through the world with dignity and grace. Sure, she was drop-dead sexy and men wanted her; but I believe it was the sweetness under the sex that really got to them. She could transform a beast into a puppy dog.

The vast majority of the men whom I've been involved with have remained my friends. I'm proud of that, and I credit Marrie Early for setting the standard. And it was also probably Marrie's take-it-as-it-comes attitude that let me get next to Gene Chandler when, in truth, I still found him less than appealing.

It was only a few days after I talked with Marrie that I ran into Gene at a Chicago radio station where I was promoting my new single. He was all excited to see me.

"Bettye LaVette," he said, "this time you just gotta let me take you to dinner."

This time I did.

Dinner was pleasant enough, even though Gene spent the entire time talking about himself. He never got over his number-one hit from 1962, "Duke of Earl." He got himself to believe that he actually *was* the Duke. Curtis Mayfield wrote some beautiful songs for Gene. Unlike Curtis, though, who had made a seamless transition into the seventies with "Superfly," Gene never had another smash like "Duke of Earl." Instead, he turned his attention to business. I saw the extent of his success when I went to his home. He was living large. I settled in with Gene and we became a short-term couple.

The most amazing thing about his place was the refrigerator. The freezer was lined with baggies of cocaine. Most people put ice cream or frozen peas in their freezer. Not Gene. He had a fortune in blow stuffed in there. His bountiful supply of high-quality coke was one of the great selling points for staying there.

At one point, we were in bed when a woman showed up. As she walked around the house, he didn't even bother to introduce me.

"Who is she?" I asked.

"One of my women," was all he said.

I got pissed. "Don't I get more respect than this?"

"What are you talking about, Bettye?"

"You got me in bed while another woman is walking through here."

"This woman's making me money. You ain't."

That was Gene Chandler, the one they called the Woman Handler. I got out of there the next day. A year later, he got busted for selling drugs and went to jail. I wasn't entirely unhappy.

The Epic episode was played out. Sales were weak. I was back in Detroit.

If it hadn't been for Jim Lewis, I might have fallen back into a barrel of blues. But Jim—constant mentor and loyal friend—always made sure I had some kind of work. It might be a union dance with a big band where I was singing jazz as if I were June Christy. It might be a trio gig at a private party with people requesting Nancy Wilson or Gloria Lynne songs. It could be work with a blues band that had me sounding like Otis Redding or Etta James. It didn't matter. I could sing anything from the Beatles to Bobby Bland. And because Jim kept hammering the importance of mastering all genres, always showing me how to read a lyric or ride over a rhythm, I was improving my artistry, even if my finances stayed flat.

It didn't take long for me to face another painful fact—the Epic episode was another instance of sugar turning to shit. The songs were good—I loved "Behind Closed Doors"—but there was no real chart action, no national recognition, nothing that would further my career in any meaningful way.

I persevered, but not without fear. If earlier in my life—at the Graystone or Small's—I had certain visions of success, there were also times, especially in the seventies, when I had visions of failure. I'd walk into a bar, order a drink, and watch a woman in her sixties singing in front of a makeshift band. She was fifty pounds overweight. Her makeup was running. Her clothes were frayed. I could hear that once upon a time her voice had been strong, but now her voice was shot. Her eyes were sad. While she sang, she worked the room, urging the patrons to stuff a dollar bill or two in her bra. Some did, but most didn't. At one point, a guy screamed, "Let's turn on the jukebox. Anything is better than this bitch!" I wanted to slug the guy. I wanted to cry. I wanted to stop seeing myself in this woman.

Would I become an old lady, begging for dollars while singing some two-bit blues in a tired voice I could no longer control? I hated that thought, but I had it. I couldn't lose it. I was getting scared.

Bettye LaVette," said Bobby Bland, my favorite of all blues singers, "you got nothing to be scared of. You as bad as anyone out there."

We were in bed after a long night of blowing coke. We blew so much that both of us forgot about sex. With Bobby, it wasn't about sex; it was about my genuine regard for a singer I loved. His manner was as smooth as his singing style. I could listen to Bobby "Blue" Bland sing all night.

The blues and its younger brother, rhythm-and-blues, are fascinating forms. Sing them rough and primitive, like Mamie or Bessie Smith, and they penetrate your soul. Sing them shyly like Billie Holiday and they creep up on you and sink into your unconscious. Sing them subtly like Ray Charles and they turn up in whatever material you touch, whether it's "Georgia" or "America the Beautiful." Sing them like Bobby Bland, and suddenly the pain in your life, no matter how deep, turns to pleasure. Bobby is able to tease the tension out of the blues. He's a highly sophisticated singer who understands that a simple form doesn't mean you can't use it to convey complex feelings. He also understands that the key to this art form, beyond the sincere expression of your heart, is taking your time. When it comes to telling the story, no one takes his time like Bobby. I can't tell you how much I love the man.

Other fabulous vocalists helped me deepen my respect for great singing. Take Philippé Wynne. Unlike Bobby, he was the opposite of cool. When he first came through the Detroit clubs in the sixties, everyone looked to avoid him. He was gawky and homely. He was overweight and overbearing. No one would let him sing—that's how annoying he was. We thought he was nothing but a goofball. Then one night he walked in and said, "Hey, I've just been signed to take G. C. Cameron's place as lead singer for the Spinners." *Say what? The Spinners? Can't be!*

But it was. It turned out that not only was Philippé Wynne a brilliant singer, he was also an original. He had his own licks. Along with Gladys Knight, he was probably the best ad-libber of all time. He gave the Spinners new energy. If you listen to "One of a Kind (Love Affair)," "Ghetto Child," "The Rubberband Man," or "Sadie," you're in the presence of one of the most unique styles in rhythm-and-blues, a genre where uniqueness is a rarity. Like Al Green, another true original, Philippé doesn't remind you of anyone. He just is.

I just was.

I was calling friends at Philly International, including Thom Bell, who'd written some of the Calla songs, to see if he could help me out. Thom never called back. I couldn't get through to guys like Kenny Gamble and Leon Huff. They were too busy, too important.

Clarence Paul always called back. Writing with Stevie Wonder and Morris Broadnax, Clarence had a hit when Aretha recorded their "Until You Come Back to Me (That's What I'm Gonna Do)." That meant Clarence had some money. If I couldn't pay the mortgage, I could always count on Clarence. And if he was lonely and looking for love, he could always count on me. I still wasn't over Clarence.

Walter Jackson was always saying he couldn't get over me. He was constantly after me. He knew I loved his voice, and he figured that, because he had had polio, he'd win my sympathy. Walter was a great singer, but that was it. I didn't desire him. That made him mad, and on the little tour we did together, he'd come offstage after a stomping, screaming standing ovation and say to me, "See, Bettye, you can't do that." He was right. At that time in my career, I couldn't get the audience reaction he did.

Muthafucka.

The seventies became Stevie Wonder's breakthrough decade. He won a thousand Grammys and became the golden boy of pop music. His albums like *Songs in the Key of Life* were huge sellers. I'd known Stevie since he was twelve. I had no reservations about asking him for help. Could I tour with him? Would he produce me? Did he have a song for me? I put in more than a couple of calls to him. I'm waiting to hear back.

Muthafucka.

. . .

In 1975, when I turned on the radio and heard Labelle doing "Lady Marmalade," I nearly slit my wrists again. That song was made for me. Except that it wasn't. It was given to Patti, who gave it the right spirit and sound. I wasn't surprised it was an across-the-board number-one hit. I was just aggravated that it wasn't *my* hit. I was still searching for mine.

Mine didn't come, which is why I turned my attention from music to men. The man who interested me most was a visiting gangster from New York who had been shot twenty times and survived. I wanted to survive. I wanted to be with big-time survivors. And if that guy happened to be going against my boyfriend at the time, the richest drug dealer in Detroit, well, I'd have to make a choice.

Sex Circus

Jack owned a dozen chicken restaurants in Harlem and dealt heroin on the side. He also had a nephew who was working out of Detroit—David—who was trying to move into the territory of the drug dealer I was seeing. I wasn't aware of the impending danger. All I knew was that Jack and David liked me when they saw me singing at a local club. After my set, they came up to me at the bar.

Jack started bragging on his nephew, talking about how, no matter how many times his enemies tried, no one could take him out.

David started bragging on his uncle, talking about how many chicken restaurants and apartment buildings he owned in Harlem and how he managed Big Maybelle and other artists like Kim Tolliver, a soul singer living in Cleveland.

I happened to mention my boyfriend at the time, the city's most prominent drug dealer.

"*Was* the city's most prominent dealer," said David.

"You need to think in terms of the future, LaVette," said Jack. "Not the past."

"Far as the future goes," David said, "that's happening in New York City. Why don't you come back with us? We're flying first class into LaGuardia tomorrow night. Got a ticket with your name on it."

I knew Jack was for real. He had a reputation. But his nephew was sketchy and flat-out crazy. He had that far-off gaze that made me wonder. The fact that he'd survived twenty attempts on his life certainly impressed me. The fact that he liked me pleased me. And besides, I wasn't making any real money in Detroit. A trip to New York might do me good. Besides, Jack had music-biz connections.

We flew off to New York. When we landed, two limos were waiting. Jack went off in one direction, and David and I went in another.

In our limo, we started doing lines. David checked us into a fancy Midtown hotel, where the party continued for several weeks. He went out during the day and at night came back with fabulous jewelry for me. He took me to the best restaurants. He took me to the Village to hear jazz. The high life kept getting higher until the night he didn't return. I didn't think much of it. It's no big deal for a man to stay out all night. After all, David wasn't exactly my husband. But one night turned into two, and two into three, and on the fourth day I discovered that my key didn't work in the door. The hotel manager was saying we had a two-thousand-dollar unpaid bill. *We?*

"Yes, you and your man."

"It's his room, not mine."

"Don't matter to me whose room it is. No one's getting in there without paying me two thousand dollars."

"All my stuff is in there."

"All your stuff is now my stuff until I get two thousand dollars."

"I don't have two thousand dollars."

"That ring and necklace you're wearing look like they can bring two thousand dollars."

"I gotta give you my jewelry to get in my room?"

"You do if you want your stuff back."

"Can you give me a minute?"

"I'll give you two."

I had some numbers for David, but no one was answering. I finally reached Jack and told him the situation.

"My nephew is a fuckup," he said. "He's disappeared. No one knows where he is, not even me."

"He's left me in the lurch," I said.

"Look, honey, get out of the hotel situation as best you can. I'll give you an address of one of my buildings up in Harlem. Go to the penthouse apartment. Got a beautiful view. You'll like it. You can stay there."

I traded my jewelry for my clothes and, without enough money for a cab, hopped the A train, the quickest way to get to Harlem. When I got to the apartment and knocked on the door, a man answered. He was wearing a woman's slip.

"Come in, sugar," he said. "Are you here for V?"

"No, I'm here 'cause Jack gave me this address."

"He wants you to stay here?"

"I think so."

"V gonna like you, baby. Come on in."

I looked around the apartment and saw a dozen gay guys from the ages of seventeen to thirty. They were watching TV, trying on clothes, reading books, napping on the couch. They looked me over from head to foot.

"V!" one of them cried. "Jack done sent you a fresh one."

The bedroom door opened and out came V—not a gay woman, but a genuine, government-inspected, prime-cut bull dyke. Arms like Popeye's, cuts all over her face, a mouth of messed-up teeth.

"Don't you worry about these sissies," said V. "They just mad they ain't cute as you. Come on in, sugar. You're safe in here."

I wondered. I worried. I still had my occasional nights with Cindy, but Cindy was cute and feminine and not threatening in the least. V was a monster. I didn't want a monster making love to me.

"Here's the deal, honey," said V. "I ain't doing nothing you don't want done."

"The thing is, I just need a place to sleep."

"You got your side of the bed, I got my mine, and if there's any action, it's gonna have to start with you."

"Thank you," I said.

"The real action," said V, "is out there in the living room. You should see what happens when Jack comes by."

It turned out that Jack was a voyeur. He showed up every night, a coke crust of white around his nose. He got the boys good and high and then got them to put on a show for him. It was a sex circus. They'd do three-ways, four-ways, this-ways, and that-ways. They were practically acrobats. I've never seen so many positions for sucking and fucking. No orifice went untouched.

Jack never got in the middle of the ring. As one of the boys sucked him off, Jack simply watched until he passed out.

After a few days, one of the gay guys just wanted to watch me. Fact is, he wanted to be me. He started dressing up in my clothes and parading around the apartment. V, who turned out to be an absolute doll, told him I was a singer and I was soon teaching him all my songs. Soon there were two Bettye LaVettes living in Jack's apartment.

During the day, the boys would go out and steal. They'd bring back mink coats and gowns, cosmetics and jewelry. V was the house mom. If any of them didn't bring back enough merchandise, V, the ferocious but friendly dyke, would slap them upside the head and bring 'em back in line.

I stayed for a few weeks. I have to admit that it was entertaining. But the gangsters who kept showing up with Jack were dangerous. The scene was fueled by endless amounts of cocaine. I felt like something was about to pop, and when it did, I wanted to be gone.

So what did I do? The usual. Called Jim Lewis.

"Jim," I said, "I fucked up again."

"Ain't surprised."

"I need to get outta here and don't have the money for a ticket home."

"Junior," he said, "when you *ever* gonna learn that you're a star. If you want people to treat you as one, you have to act like one."

"I don't need a lecture, just a plane ticket."

"I'll get you the ticket."

"And work? I haven't sung in months."

"I got something that might keep you for a while."

"Something permanent?"

"As permanent as a band funded by a numbers man can be."

"My own band?"

"Led by Rudy Robinson."

"That's great."

"I even have a name."

"Something better than Bettye and Her Boys, I presume."

"Much better—Seven Below Zero."

"Is that the temperature I'm coming home to, Jim?"

"Cold front coming in from Canada. But this band's so hot, you'll feel like it's June."

"Bless you, Daddy."

"I'll see you at the airport, baby."

Jim pulled off the coup. The man was always pulling off coups, and all out of regard for me. What had I done to deserve this kind of treatment? I know he loved my talent and saw me as a serious student who had learned his lessons. Great teachers thrive on serious students, but Jim had deep kindness in his heart and felt my need for a professional ally. He had seen how all these record companies had dropped me for no reason. He knew the heartache I experienced and wanted in the worst way to make up for it. That's why I'll love him forever.

He helped me put together a couple of bands. The first had been The Fun Company. But Seven Below Zero sounded so hip that, even though I was still far from the big time, I was in good musical shape playing local gigs making minor money. I was back home with Mama, Sister, and my daughter, now a smart and lovely teenager.

Maybe the local grind would lead to something. Maybe one of

the big-shot execs I'd known through the years—Ahmet Ertegun or Jerry Wexler—would return my calls. Maybe they'd finally find a hit song for me. Maybe they'd offer me a production budget, a top-flight studio, and a hot producer.

But the phone stayed silent, and the small gigs stayed small.

Sometimes old friends from New York would check in. One was Don Gardner's bass player.

"Bettye LaVette," he said. "This is Win."

"Hey, baby, you in New York?"

"I am. Married Debbie Allen."

"I didn't know that. That's beautiful."

"The thing is, they wanted Debbie for the national company of *Bubbling Brown Sugar*. But it's more a singing part than a dancing part, so naturally I thought of you."

"That's so sweet, Win. But if there's any dancing, I'm not a good choice."

"Oh come on, Bettye, you got your dance moves. Can I have the director call you?"

"A call can't hurt."

The call came an hour later.

"Yes," said the director. "It's mainly singing. It's a musical revue and you'll have four featured numbers. But there is dancing."

"What kind of dancing?"

"Tap."

"I'm out."

"You can tap."

"I can't."

"Of course you can."

"Look, you can't just call someone up and say you can tap. It doesn't work that way. I can't do it." And I hung up.

Five minutes later, the director was back on the phone. I don't know what made him so persistent. "I'm sending you a plane ticket. Come to New York and we'll teach you to tap."

"I'm unteachable."

"It's easy."

"Promise?"

"Promise."

It turned out to be one of the hardest things I've ever done.

Bubbling

When I arrived in New York, I stayed with my friend singer Jean Dushon and her husband. They helped me get through the tap-dancing ordeal, giving me pointers and, after the arduous rehearsals, even washing and massaging my feet.

Beyond being inept, I felt silly. Throwing my hands up in the air and jumping all around, I felt like some rag doll. I had a complex, but I didn't give up. I stayed. I learned. And I got the part.

The part was good. There was no real story, just an excuse to see dances and hear songs loosely connected with the Harlem Renaissance of the twenties and thirties. It opened on Broadway in 1976 and ran for 766 performances. When I joined the national touring company in the summer of 1977, it was an established hit.

Once I got past the trauma of tapping, I was thoroughly

thrilled. This was what I had imagined show business to be all about—you put on a fabulous costume, sing a song or two, receive a standing ovation, and then go to a chic bar to sip champagne with your sophisticated friends. I thought I was Ginger Rogers. Of course, Ginger could dance, but she couldn't sing "God Bless the Child," "Sweet Georgia Brown," "(In My) Solitude," and "Stormy Monday" like I could. I had no problems when I replaced Vivian Reed from the original production. I had big moments and took advantage of them. As Jim Lewis had so patiently taught me, I drained the drama out of every song. Because of his tireless training, I commanded the stage. I reveled in the spotlight. At thirty-one, after a lifetime of corner bars and sleazy juke joints, I was ready for legitimate theater.

The star of the show was Charles "Honi" Coles. He had danced with the Cab Calloway band in the forties before forming the famous duo of Coles & Atkins. His partner, Cholly Atkins, was the man hired by Berry Gordy in the sixties to teach all his acts—the Temps, Tops, Supremes, and Vandellas—to dance for their gigs at the Copacabana.

The fact that Honi was thirty-five years older than I was made absolutely no difference. I adored him. He was sweet as honey and reminded me of my beloved Clarence Paul. Honi was the one who showed me the nuance of tap dancing. He was a master. After working with me for a week, I was ready to take him to bed.

"I'm too old," he said.

"No, you're not, baby. Old is good."

"When you turn fifty, I'll be eighty-five. I won't be able to fuck."

"I'll help you."

"You'll leave me for a young man."

"Never. I'll be yours forever."

"I already have a wife. She's a beauty. She was in the Cotton Club chorus line."

"Doesn't matter."

"But I could never leave her."

"Why not?"

"She makes the best spaghetti."

"I'll learn to make it better."

"But I have a mistress who was also in the Cotton Club line. Been with her as long as I've been with my wife."

"You mean I'd be number three?"

"At best." He laughed.

I kissed him, saying that I'd stand in line for him anytime. We became the best of friends. We went on the road for nine months where he regaled me with fabulous showbiz stories—how he worked on Broadway in the original *Gentlemen Prefer Blondes* at the Ziegfeld Theatre with twenty-eight-year-old Carol Channing and choreographer Agnes de Mille.

As the national touring company made its way around the country, I fell into a satisfying routine. Nine months into it, though, I received a bad shock—Honi was leaving to do a show in Paris.

"Take me with you, Daddy!" I begged.

"Wish I could, Bettye, but they need you here."

"I'm replaceable," I said. "You aren't."

"Are you kidding? They got Cab Calloway taking my place."

"Cab's cool, but he can't dance like you."

"Cab has other virtues."

"Will I like him?" I asked Honi.

"No, but he'll like you."

As it turned out, I did like Cab—but no one else in the company did.

He was in his seventies and cantankerous as hell—so cranky, in fact, that no one wanted to work with him. I had a different point of view. To me, Cab Calloway was show business history, and I was honored to work with him. Besides, he had the best stories. I liked how he had something bad to say about everyone. And he did take a liking to me.

He liked me so much that I was the only one he'd listen to. That's why the cast voted me the equity deputy, the leader of the actors. First I had to tell him that he couldn't wear his signature white suit for the entire show. We wore white in the last act, and if he wore white earlier, the effect would be ruined.

Cab didn't give a shit. "Been wearing white before those assholes were born," he said. "Why should I change?"

"It'll help the show, Cab," I said.

"Fuck the show."

"You *are* the show. You wanna do everything to keep it going."

"All right, tell them to get me a blue suit."

The next day I brought him a blue suit. He ran his hand over the fabric and said, "It's cheap. I ain't wearing cheap shit like this."

Costume lady found another suit with a finer fabric.

"That shade of blue is too dull," said Cab. "Get an electric blue that the audience can see. I need to be *seen*."

During one of the performances, he stuck out his foot and tripped one of the dancers. She wasn't hurt, but she could have been. She wanted to bring charges and I had to talk her out of it.

When the show moved on to another city, I was the only one he let ride with him in his town car. We had to stop every hundred miles so I could run in and put down his bets at the OTB machines. I didn't mind. I liked how he complimented me.

"Look at how those bitches dress when they're offstage," he said. "They got rollers in their hair. They're wearing sweatpants and baggy T-shirts and raggedy slippers on their feet. But you, Bettye LaVette, you get dressed up every day 'cause you know what it means to be a star."

"I do?"

"Yes, ma'am, you sure do. That's why I let you ride with me."

We had dinner together every night. I'd ply him with questions. One night I asked him about Duke Ellington.

"Couldn't stand the muthafucka," he said.

"Why not?"

"Egomaniac."

"Well, Cab . . ."

"I know, I got an ego too. But, see, Duke was jealous of me. I had my shit together before he did. And I was a big star. Bigger audience. Made bigger bread."

"But he was a brilliant writer."

"That was Billy Strayhorn. Billy was the brilliant writer—and he was Duke's ghostwriter. While Billy was downstairs in the band room writing 'Satin Doll,' Duke was up in his bedroom with two or three of them satin dolls."

"You sound jealous."

"Duke was fair-skinned. Not as fair as me, but in those days fair skin got you any gal you wanted. That's why Basie was jealous of us both. He was darker."

"But I'm sure he got his fair share of ladies."

"Not the prime pick, my dear."

"You weren't jealous of Duke and Count because they had royal names and you didn't, were you?"

"You're funny, little missy, you just say those things to provoke me. But I've got nothing to be jealous about. Duke's six feet under the ground, and I'm the star of a show and having dinner with a beautiful lady like you."

"Keep talking, Cab."

On our night off in San Francisco, Cab and I went to see Peggy Lee at the Venetian Room in the Fairmont Hotel on Nob Hill. Jim Lewis liked Peggy. He thought of her as a singer who did the most with a small voice. Jim said it wasn't about volume or power; it was about dynamics. He not only praised her ability to phrase with great subtlety, but instructed me to appreciate her sense of drama. Back in the late sixties, when I heard her do "Is That All There Is"—written and produced by Leiber and Stoller, the guys I had always wanted to produce me—it was another wrist-slitting moment. Given the chance, I know I could have killed that song.

Peggy certainly killed it. In the high-class environment of a cabaret club like the Venetian Room, she was at her best. The feeling was intimate. She was in your face in a way that made you love the lady even more. Sitting there, I wondered if, in a million years, I'd get a chance to play a club like this, where the hefty cover charge meant that patrons were willing to pay dearly for the privilege to hear you and only you. Peggy's audience listened with rapt attention. I was envious.

. . .

On the other side of the cultural divide, disco was at its height. It was 1978, and Donna Summer was red hot with "Last Dance" and "MacArthur Park." Candi Staton had hit with "Young Hearts Run Free" and Gloria Gaynor would soon top the charts with "I Will Survive." I was no fan of disco, but if I had been given an anthem like "Ring My Bell" and made a quick million, I would not have complained.

At the same time, at age thirty-two I didn't see myself as a disco diva. I was something of a Broadway star—and that was fine by me. I knew I could outsing ninety-nine percent of the disco dames out there, but the music didn't interest me. It was monotonous, formulaic, and, for the most part, silly bullshit.

Then one day disco came my way in the form of nineteen-year-old Cory Robbins, who said that he and his partner had a track they wanted me to dub my voice over. It was called "Doin' the Best That I Can." I recorded it for West End Records without much thought. After a few days, I left the city with one of the *Bubbling* road companies. When I returned a month later, Cory called.

"'Doin' the Best That I Can' is a disco favorite, but it's about to get even bigger."

"Why is that?" I asked.

"Because Walter Gibbons is about to remix it."

Gibbons was famous in the disco world. His remix was mainly an instrumental with my vocal buried somewhere two-thirds through what seemed like an hour-long song. He invited me to sing in one of those barnlike Manhattan gay clubs where the boys were popping pills and making merry. I had heard the version once, but I didn't remember how long the instrumental introduction was. I didn't even know when to start singing. My performance was a mess, but the boys were too fucked up to notice. For a night, I was a disco diva. Years later I saw that the remix made a list of best disco songs, a fact that does not fill me with pride. The result of all this, though, was the same one I had been seeing since I started out singing sixteen years earlier: no royalties.

In this same dizzy disco period, I was in New York, getting ready to take off with *Bubbling* again for two weeks of performances in Chicago, when I ran into a friend. Just like the movie says, it happened on Forty-second Street.

I walked into Arnie Geller, who I knew from the world of Detroit TV when, for a short time, I had hosted a local show, *Swingin' Time.*

"Holy shit," he said. "Bettye LaVette! This is providential. You're the gal I need to see!"

Arnie said he was working with Steve Buckingham in Atlanta.

"Who's he?"

"Hottest producer in the country."

"Who's he produced?"

"Alicia Bridges. Steve and I are co-managing her. Her 'I Love the Nightlife' is the number-one record in the world. You've heard it, haven't you?"

"Sure, I've heard it."

"You like it?"

"It's catchy."

"Anyway, he mentioned you the other day. He has this writer, Buddy Buie, who wrote that famous song 'Stormy' that you recorded."

"I remember, but nothing happened with my version."

"Doesn't matter. They played it for Steve and he flipped. Buie has some new songs for you. Steve wants to produce."

"Well, the thing is, I got this little contract with West End Records."

"Get out of it."

"I'll try."

"Don't try, Bettye, do it. This is the big time, girl. No one's hotter than Steve Buckingham. With Buie's songs, you're gonna be bigger than Donna Summer."

I should have known better, but how could I stop dreaming the impossible dream? How could I not believe this was the sure-enough break I'd been waiting for? How could I give up hope and fall into despair? I couldn't. I wouldn't.

I went to West End.

"Release me," I said.

"Fine, but no royalties on anything you've recorded for us."

Stupidly, I agreed. I didn't know that over the years "Doin' the Best That I Can" would grow into a dance-floor staple and turn into a considerable seller. My eyes were on the prize in the sky, the writers of "Stormy," the managers of Alicia Bridges, the hot producer in Atlanta.

I went down to Atlanta and met Steve, who had a couple of songs for me. One was "Tell Me a Lie," a nice, medium-tempo thing asking a married man to pretend he isn't. We cut the songs. Steve loved the way they turned out. I did too. And then—you've heard this before, I've heard this before, *everyone's* heard this before—the sugar turned to shit.

Buzzard luck.

Geller disappeared. Buddy Buie disappeared. The promises faded. The songs never came out.

"Can you tell me why?" I asked Steve.

"Wish I could," he said.

"Tell me a lie," I said. "Ain't that the name of the song?"

"I guess so."

I *knew* so. Another heartbreak, yet not nearly as great as the heartbreak waiting for me back home in Detroit.

Sister

I adored my father. Mama got on my nerves, but she was a wonderful mother and a great supporter. She raised my daughter and let me live the life of an entertainer. It was sister Mattie, though, who was really my heart. I've never admired anyone more.

Sister never had it easy. As a teenager, she married a dog. Her second man was a pig and a brute. He beat her constantly. I can't explain why a woman as wonderful as Sister allowed men to mistreat her so often and for so long. I know she didn't feel beautiful because she was skinny. In those days, skinny wasn't sexy. For all her intelligence and grace, all her kindness and compassion, she felt inferior.

I cherish the memories of taking Sister on the road. We once traveled with the Temptations and I was thrilled to see her flirting with Paul Williams. She was with me on another tour when we ran out of money and were put out of our hotel. I knew of an apartment building that was essentially a headquarters for whores and decided to take her there.

"Don't be shocked, Sister," I said, knowing she'd lived a sheltered life. "But we'll be staying with a group of working ladies."

By the end of that first week, all the prostitutes were coming to Sister with their problems. She'd become their official counselor, patiently listening to their tales of woe and soothing their hurt feelings. Sister was something else.

In addition to helping our mother care for my daughter, Sister always worked. For years she had a job at a laundry. She taught me to iron and starch a white shirt with absolute perfection, a skill I still value. Sister did everything just so. She was a perfectionist. She always encouraged me to do what I wanted without, as she put it, "losing the semblance of being a mother."

Sister lived her life out of romance books. I hated how she never had the opportunity to be loved, adored, or even appreciated. She never had money or got to enjoy even the most minimal luxury.

Because Sister had avoided the excessive lifestyle of show business, I expected her to outlive me. She suffered from high blood pressure but told me that the doctors had it under control. So when the call came, I fell into a state of shock.

I was at the Paramus Theater in New Jersey. The Saturday matinee of *Bubbling* had just ended. Jim was on the phone.

"I hate to tell you this, Bettye," he said, "but Sister has passed."

Sister! That couldn't be. I had talked to her the night before. We had talked for hours about my latest romance. As usual, she had been beautifully patient in letting me express my heart. We talked till the wee small hours of the morning. Finally, Sister said,

"You better get your rest. You've got your matinee to do and I have my waitress job."

Those were her last words to me.

I came home to bury Sister, gone at forty-six. I was thirty-three and Terrye was eighteen. I believe it was tougher on Terrye than on anyone else. She had lost her surrogate mama, a woman far closer to her than I was.

At our small memorial service, Rudy Robinson played two of Sister's favorite songs—"Staying Alive" and "Giving Up." Terrye prepared Sister's makeup. I could never have done that. I couldn't look. I never have and never will look into an open casket. I have no memories of anyone's dead body. My memories are all of the living.

Going back to work the next day was hard. I had already broken my vow to my understudy to never allow her to take my place—and I didn't want to break the promise again. I left Detroit knowing that without Sister, my life would never be the same. I had lost my biggest supporter and my best friend.

Bubbling went on for years. I grew tired of touring, but the songs were good and the pay steady. It was, in fact, the only steady pay I'd ever known.

I'd failed to make any money in the lucrative age of disco, and that was all right with me. Disco was not a friend to the true rhythm-and-blues artist. It thrived on superficiality and half-ass singing. Those last years of the seventies offered me next to nothing. It wasn't that I didn't like the music. Chaka Khan was coming on and Chaka could certainly sing. Teddy Pendergrass was a strong presence, and I was glad that my lifelong friends the O'Jays had a smash with "Use ta Be My Girl." I would have loved to have had a deal from Gamble and Huff at Philly International. I knew many of the music moguls in charge, but none of them called. I wasn't shy about calling Al Bell, for example, who had a big career at many labels. He used to chase after me when, as a teen, I was singing "My Man." But, as an adult, when I asked to speak to him, his secretary put me on hold. I'm still holding. Muthafucka.

So I went on from city to city, *Bubbling* my way through life. It was only when we checked into the Hyatt in Louisville, Kentucky, that something changed for me. And I know you won't be surprised to learn that the change had to do with a man.

I remember calling cousin Margaret back in Detroit.

"What's new, Betty Jo?" she asked.

"Nothing much. Except that I'm getting married."

"WHAT!"

"You heard me."

"Is it someone I know?"

"No, I met him here in Louisville."

"You've only been in Louisville a week."

"How long does it take to know a man?"

"A lot longer than a goddamn week," said Margaret.

"Well, it took me less than a week."

"Why in hell are you getting married?"

"One of the reasons is that he's gorgeous."

"What's this gorgeous man's name?"

"Donnie Sadler."

"And what's this gorgeous man's age?"

"Maybe twenty-six."

"So he's seven years younger than you."

"Anything wrong with that?" I asked.

"Not if he has a job. Is the man working?"

"He sure is. He works for the Hyatt hotel."

"Parking cars?"

"Please, Margaret. Give me a little credit. He's the front desk manager. And he's in their executive program. He's on his way up."

"Oh, Lord," my cousin said in exasperation. "You done lost your mind again."

"No, I found the man I've been looking for. And I can't tell you how crazy he is about me."

"You don't have to."

"Anyway, I want you to help me put the wedding together."

"Wedding! Y'all are already talking about an actual wedding? When?"

"Before the show ends its run. I want to get married onstage."

"Oh, Lord."

Donnie was wonderful. Beyond his fabulous looks, he was a gentleman from Philadelphia, a man with a plan for a bright future. Everyone in the *Bubbling* cast loved him. He had the kind of personality that wanted to please everyone. Determined to be successful, he had a good grasp of Hyatt's corporate culture. He was also stable and, unlike me, not in the least bit crazy. I never really had gone with an ambitious, legitimate businessman with no connections to show business. The change was refreshing. The lovemaking was satisfying. The deal was sealed.

The wedding itself happened onstage before one of the performances of *Bubbling*. Cab Calloway gave me away.

"Your husband," said Cab, "is nearly as handsome as I was when I was his age. What age is that, eighteen?"

"No, he's older than that, Cab."

"Whatever his age, you found a pretty one."

While we took the wedding vows, the company's dancers did a ballet. It couldn't have been more beautiful.

Margaret was so undone by the idea of my marriage to a man I barely knew that she kept changing outfits in the dressing room. Fact is, she never made it out of the dressing room; she missed the wedding altogether. When she finally showed up at the party, I asked where she had been.

"I guess I just couldn't watch," she said.

"Margaret, I have every intention of living happily ever after."

"I give it a year," she said.

"You're wrong."

She was, but, on the deepest level, she was right.

This was the start of the eighties, a new decade, a new life for me. I had a gorgeous young husband. I had a different lifestyle, following him to where his work took him. I had a man who could provide for me. I had a drama-free situation.

And yet, looking back, I think I probably wanted out of the marriage a week after my wedding. I fought that feeling and for a long time hid it from Donnie. I tried to make a go of the marriage and, as you'll see, spent time in cities I disliked, all to prove that Donnie was up to the task of being married to me when, in fact, he wasn't. I spent a lot of time trying to figure out how to extricate myself from the situation without hurting him. But Donnie was fundamentally so decent a man that I couldn't do anything that might undercut him. So I stayed, even when I knew I had made a mistake in making this lifelong commitment.

The commitment took me to New Orleans, where Donnie would be head of housekeeping for the Hyatt hotel just outside the French Quarter. In that same Hyatt, pianist Ellis Marsalis—father to the famous Marsalis sons and a patron saint of Crescent City jazz—had a big band that played the Sunday brunch. When I asked if I could sing "Moon River," he agreed, and the next thing I knew I had a gig with Ellis. Not long after that, Phil Parnell, a great talent who had just graduated from the Berklee College of Music in Boston, came home to New Orleans. It was the return of the prodigal son. He came by the Hyatt, heard me, and recruited me to take the place of his recently divorced singer-wife.

We formed a band and got a gig at the Absinthe Bar on Bourbon Street in the heart of the French Quarter. I played there for a while, as well as other spots, but was never really comfortable in New Orleans, where I was repulsed by the racial bigotry. I remember being asked to sing at a fancy event hosted by one of the city's dowagers, a woman with an aristocratic bearing. I was interested in meeting her. She looked like a character out of a movie from the thirties.

"Where are you from, my dear?" she asked.

"Detroit," I said.

"Oh, well, my mistake. I presumed you were just another local coon."

I was too shocked to haul off and deck her. Instead, I just stood there, shaking my head in disbelief. "Fuck you, lady" would have been too mild a response. The I-wish-you-were-dead look in my eyes said more.

After five or six months of gigging around New Orleans, I

had one promoter say to me, "Bettye LaVette, the consensus of most of the club owners on Bourbon Street is that you are an uppity nigger."

"Tell those muthafuckas they are absolutely right. I'm glad they see me for who I am."

Who was I?

Mrs. Donnie Sadler. Ms. Bettye LaVette. Freelance singer, able to render the finest jazz, rock, or rhythm-and-blues at the occasion of your choice. Big voice, big attitude, eclectic repertoire, emotional delivery. Striking stage appearance. Looks good in a gown or jeans and a sweater. In shape. Great stage banter. Funny, funky, and sophisticated. Recorded more than sixty songs with the biggest record labels in America.

How many albums? you ask.

None.

Not one single goddamn album.

Until now. Until 1981, the year that I was living with my beautiful Donnie in New Orleans, the year that, out of nowhere, I get a call from Steve Buckingham.

"Bettye," he said, "I've got good news."

"I love good news," I said. "I love great news even better. And the best news of all concerns me getting money."

He laughed and said, "Then you'll love this news. Diana Ross has left Motown for RCA."

"Why should I care?"

"Because that leaves an open slot in their roster for a female singer."

"And I'm going to replace Diane Ross? I'm going to be signed by the label that for the past twenty years never wanted anything to do with me?"

"That's right."

"When was the last time you went to a psychiatrist to get your meds checked, Steve?"

"My mental health is strong, Bettye, and so is your voice. And this is no joke. This is a done deal. Not a singles deal. An *album* deal."

"That Berry Gordy has approved?"

"I didn't need Berry for this. Lee Young is in charge, and he's one of your biggest fans. He's committed to a Bettye LaVette album."

"I need to hear it from the man himself. Have him call me."

A half-hour later, Lee Young did just that.

"We'd love to have you on Motown," he said. "I've been listening to your records over the years and never thought you were given the chance you deserve."

"Mr. Young," I said, "I think I have fallen deeply and permanently in love with you."

Lee laughed, and said, "Look, Bettye, Motown needs a mature female vocalist, and you're it. There's no one better. Steve wants you in Nashville next month. I'm sending you a first-class ticket and expecting a Grammy-winning album."

"And this is really, truly Motown?" I asked.

"Berry's office is right down the hall from me."

"And he knows about this?"

"Knows and approves."

"And won't kill it at the last minute?"

"I'll guarantee you that you'll have a Motown album in your hands by the end of the year."

That's all I needed to hear from a high-ranking Motown executive. I was in, I was ready, I was about to record my first album on my hometown label that had left my hometown for Hollywood only to reach out to me in New Orleans to send me to Nashville.

Steve Buckingham had become one of Clive Davis's go-to producers at Arista. He was coming off big successes with Melissa Manchester and Dionne Warwick. He demanded and got a good budget for our record. He sent me dozens of songs and let me pick the ones I could relate to. We decided to re-record "Tell Me a Lie"—the version we cut in Atlanta never came out—in addition to a Sam Dees tune, "Right in the Middle (Of Falling in Love)," which became the first single. Steve hired a string section for a ballad, "Before I Even Knew Your Name (I Needed You)" by Steve Dorff. I was excited to do Dorff's song. He was a writer of TV and movie themes, and even more important, this tune required a soft and gentle voice. I wanted to prove to Jim Lewis I could sing with restraint and femininity—and did just that.

The lyrics were perfect. When I sent them to Jim, he said, "Yes, that's pretty much what I was talking about." For good measure, we included a couple of Motown standards—"I Heard It Through the Grapevine" and "If I Were Your Woman."

I brought cousin Margaret to Nashville, where she spent all her time reading the newspaper. The sessions didn't please me entirely. I didn't like being told to restrain my style. I felt like I was being held back. I didn't see the point.

"I agree," said Lee Young, when he heard the tapes. "I love your voice and your voice isn't being given free rein. But don't worry about it. I know you can do a much better album than this—and you will. The point of this record is to let everyone know that you're back. For your next album, there'll be no compromises—you'll handpick the producer and the material."

I took Lee at his word. A compromise this time was okay, especially since Kramer and Kramer, a major agency, had agreed to start booking me. More than anything, though, I just wanted to see an album with my picture on the cover—which was when the sugar started turning to shit.

When the proof of the cover came in the mail I was back in New Orleans. I ripped open the envelope. The title was the one we had decided on, *Tell Me a Lie*. But, much to my horror, my picture was not on the cover. The photo showed another woman being embraced by a black man in the process of removing his wedding ring. She looked white. I went nuts. I called the label. Lee Young wasn't there. Some junior executive took the call.

"We had a long photo shoot," I said. "There were dozens of good pictures of me. So why the hell is another woman in this picture?"

"Because everyone knows you were recently married," said this idiot, "and we concluded that showing you with a married man wouldn't go over."

"You're kidding," I said.

"No, I'm serious."

"That is some of the dumbest shit I ever heard in my life. First of all, my marriage wasn't exactly national news. And even if it was, people don't exactly look at me like I'm Mary Poppins. Besides, why not just use a picture of me by myself? That's more appropriate anyway."

"They've already been printed and shipped."

"Without my approval?"

No answer on the other end.

The next day, Lee Young answered my call.

"You gotta do something about this, Lee," I said. "My first album and some other woman's picture is on the cover. That's not right."

"I couldn't agree more," he said.

"Then you'll stop the presses."

"I can't stop anything."

"Why not?"

"I'm no longer with the company."

"No."

"Yes. Berry's bringing in Raynoma Singleton."

"His ex-wife?"

"The same."

"The one who's been fighting him for years."

"I'm afraid so."

"The one who will have absolutely no interest in promoting my album?"

"That's my fear."

"So the album is dead on arrival."

"I feel terrible, Bettye, I really do."

"I know you do, Lee, and I can't blame you. I can only thank you. Without you, I wouldn't have my first album, even if it doesn't have my picture on the cover."

"I'm still hoping the record does something."

"I am too."

But I knew in my heart that it wouldn't.

And it didn't.

To make matters worse, Kramer and Kramer dropped me without explanation or apology.

Muthafuckas.

. . .

So what happens now?
    "Tired of New Orleans?" Donnie asked me.

"Yes, baby," I said. "Very tired."

"Well, then, I've got good news."

"I could use a little."

"Hyatt's transferring me. Making me the manager of a hotel."

"Where?"

"Fort Worth."

"Fort Worth, Texas?"

"Yes."

I didn't say anything.

"You don't sound excited, baby," Donnie said.

"That's 'cause I'm not."

"You will be once we get there."

Except that I wasn't.

Trance

Marrie Early had gone through some changes. She had become a Jehovah's Witness. She had also experienced the tragic death of a child. Convinced that modern medicine was incompatible with her new religious beliefs, she refused to take the baby to the doctor. She was certain prayer would work. It didn't, and the child died. Yet for all that she suffered, Marrie was always there for me as a loyal and loving friend. She never lost track of me or failed to call.

"Hey, Bettye," she said on the phone, "I want to hear how you're doing in Texas."

"I'm plotting to get out."

"So I gather you don't like it."

"The word is *hate*, Marrie."

"What about Donnie?"

"The word is *boring*."

"But he's a good man, isn't he?"

"A beautiful guy, but I'm trapped in this boring life."

"You gigging?"

"In Fort Worth there's no one to sing to except the cows. I've started an exercise class in the apartment complex where we live."

"So you're staying in shape."

"Marrie, I'm always in shape. But what for? I'm going stir-crazy in godforsaken Texas."

"How much longer do you think you can hang in there, baby?" she asked.

"About an hour."

"Oh, come on, you've got more patience than that."

"This place is sapping whatever patience I might have had. Texas is more racist than Mississippi."

"You can't lose heart, Bettye. Something good's gonna happen—and it's gonna happen soon."

A month later, something happened that at first didn't seem good at all. Donnie lost his job at the Hyatt. Suddenly, we were both down on our luck. Where would we go now? The only place that made sense was Detroit. At least I had a house in Detroit that was paid for.

The car I'd bought with my Motown money had been repossessed, so we packed up all our shit and put it in a U-Haul that broke down halfway between Texas and Michigan. I was falling out of love by the minute. Somehow we made it to Detroit.

Bad fortune turned good when a black-owned corporation

bought the famous Book-Cadillac Hotel in downtown Detroit. They were only too happy to have Donnie, a college graduate with extensive experience, manage the property.

The Book-Cadillac was an apt metaphor for the state of my marriage and career as I headed into the mid-eighties and age forty. The hotel was built in the twenties at the corner of Michigan Avenue and Washington Boulevard in downtown Detroit. Designed like an Italian Renaissance palace, it was an architectural jewel, redone in the thirties and modernized in the fifties. By the seventies, along with the rest of the city, the hotel had fallen into disrepair. When, in the aftermath of its restoration, Donnie came to manage it in 1983, there was new hope. The Book-Cadillac was coming back. I was coming back. All was not lost.

Donnie moved into the home I still owned and where Mama and Terrye, now a grown woman, still lived. My original support group, led by the ever loyal Jim Lewis, was still in place. Donnie helped in every possible way. He gave cousin Margaret a good job at the hotel. He gave my friend George Richardson a cleaning contract so lucrative that George was able to buy another dry cleaner location and two vans. He also booked me in the hotel's nightclub for a long-term engagement.

On an even happier note, my return home made me realize that, for the first time in some twenty years, I was over Clarence Paul. I think that happened when I made the ill-fated Motown record. Singing those Motown songs, I realized that my obsession had finally run its course. I didn't seek him out, didn't dream of him, didn't fantasize that one day he'd see the truth, sweep me up in his arms, and carry me off to paradise. I'd always have a special place for Clarence in my pantheon of men, but that was it. My crazy love was spent.

While my own career was going nowhere fast, I could celebrate the success of my friends with a grateful heart. Tina Turner's triumph as a solo artist was beautiful. It was nearly as good as if it had happened to me. I felt that it *could* happen to me. Her cover of "Let's Stay Together" followed by "What's Love Got to Do with It" were hits and proof that she could do it alone.

When Marvin Gaye, who had been hitless after "Got to Give It Up," came back with "Sexual Healing," I was also thrilled. I loved it when he got his first Grammy. I'd lost track of Marvin, and through other people's accounts, I came to realize that the guy I had known so well in Detroit—easygoing, charmingly relaxed, funny as hell—had changed. He had gone through some terrible battles of the soul. I never knew the disturbed Marvin. I'm glad I didn't know that man. I cling to the memory of the lighthearted Marvin with his mellow approach to life. Obviously, his life had turned topsy-turvy. On April Fool's Day, 1984, when Clarence Paul called to say that Marvin had been shot to death by his preacher father, I cried for my dear friend; I also couldn't help but think about the dark side of religion and what it can do to the human mind.

My mind was on my own emotional survival. Donnie's gig at the Book-Cadillac was fine, but his health was not. He was showing early signs of multiple sclerosis, a shock to everyone. For a while, we coped as best we could.

I read in the paper that famed producer Barry Hankerson was putting on a play in Detroit. Clifford Fears, Katherine Dunham's premier dancer and a local Detroiter, was the choreographer and Ron Milner, a great Detroit playwright, was doing the script. Naturally, I went to audition. I was received enthusiastically. When Jim Lewis called Clifford and Ron to encourage my being cast, they said they were creating a special character for me. Donnie provided the rehearsal space—the grand ballroom of the Book-Cadillac—and we were all set.

My character sang a gospel song, "Have You Tried Jesus?" Well, not really. And maybe it was my agnosticism that did the show in, because, after nine months of rehearsals, it opened and closed in a week. Where's Jesus when you need him?

Bettye," said the guy on the other end of the phone, "it's Steve Buckingham. I'm calling to apologize."

After my Buckingham-produced *Tell Me a Lie* Motown album disappeared without a trace, this was the first time I'd heard from Steve.

"I feel terrible," he went on. "The album was great and should have been your breakthrough."

"Where have I heard that before?"

"I mean it. I should have been in touch before this, but I've been busy."

"Wish I could say the same thing."

"But I'm not just calling to apologize, I'm calling because I have a track that needs your vocal."

"What kind of track?"

"A dance track. I call it 'Trance Dance.' Will you come down to Nashville and sing it?"

Why not? What else did I have to do? The track had a post-disco Chic feel to it. In terms of hit potential, I thought it was a day late and a dollar short. Unfortunately, I was right. It became another one of those Bettye LaVette oddities—a song no one remembers. Steve went on to a brilliant career. He produced a bunch of records and became writing partners with Dolly Parton. They had a number-one hit, "Rockin' Years," and all sorts of platinum records. That's the period when Steve's power in the record industry was at its height. That's also when I was hoping to hear from him again—but I didn't.

Muthafucka.

The matter of my marriage weighed heavily on my mind. Donnie's condition was deteriorating. He was a good man and there was no reason why he shouldn't be taken care of. But I couldn't see myself in the role of caretaker. I had to level with him.

"We've barely been married five years," I said, "and it's been rough going."

"What are you saying?"

"I'm saying that I haven't been happy."

"Was it something I did?" he asked.

"No. You've done all you could. You've been working in the hotel business. You've had to go where you were sent."

I didn't tell him that I was disappointed that he hadn't really performed in the corporate culture as I had expected. I thought by now he'd be the manager of a major hotel in New York, Paris, or Rome. But this wasn't the time to say that. He was sick and needed help.

"You've told me that your condition is never gonna get better," I said.

"It's not."

"That's why I think you need to go home to Philly."

"Home?"

"To your mom and dad. They're the only ones who can take

care of you and give you what you need. I hope I'm not sounding cold, Donnie."

"You've always been honest, Bettye. I appreciate that. I understand what you're saying. And I don't wanna be a burden to you."

"I just don't think I can do it. I wasn't made to devote all my time and energy to a husband. I respect other women who can do that, but I can't lie and tell you that I can."

"I'm always gonna love you," he said.

"I'll always love you too, but I can't be with you anymore."

A few days later, with all sorts of mixed emotions, I drove him to the airport. He was leaving me and Detroit for good. I was guilty, I was relieved, I was regretful, I was hopeful, I was experiencing every feeling under the sun.

I must give Donnie credit. He heard me loud and clear. He left without drama. No pleading, no crying, no fits, no harsh words. He flew back to New Orleans, where he thought he could make it on his own. Donnie was the straightest guy in the world except for his love of cocaine. Back down in Louisiana, that love, combined with his failing health, fucked him over. He got strung out on crack and finally did what I had suggested—he went home to Philly and let his parents care for him.

But all that was in the future. In the present, after dropping him off at the Detroit airport, I stopped at the Fairlane mall, bought a real tight black dress and a fur coat, and went out to have a good time.

Not long after I said good-bye to Donnie, another good-bye filled me with sadness. In 1989, my mentor Jim Lewis died at the age of sixty-seven.

Although we'd enjoyed an early romantic dalliance, the physical part of our affair had stopped years before. Our musical affair never stopped. Even today I never go onstage without thinking of Jim. I never approach a song without Jim in mind. I can't read a lyric without remembering what Jim taught me about singing.

"You caress a song," he said, "you don't attack it. You relax and let the song come to you. You dramatize the story like a great actress in a classic film. You take your time. You consider every word, every note. You offer the composition the dignity it deserves. You turn a phrase with subtlety and grace. You never ignore dynamics. You never stop calibrating your volume. Your intuitive feel for melody will tell you when it's time to sing with heartbreaking softness or explosive power. You have it all, you silly bitch, it's just a question of learning how to use it."

Jim taught me how to use it. The man taught me how to sing. Without him, I would never have found the professional strength to endure. He did so much more than get me thousands of gigs around Detroit that kept me from fading away completely. He was protective. He was fatherly.

"How can you be a lady," he'd ask, "when you're always on the verge of running off with some bass player or bouncer?"

Jim Lewis took a wiseass, stubborn kid and turned her into a singer. He was a lion trainer. He was a lion tamer. I can't think of anyone else who could have trained and tamed me the way he did.

I miss Jim and Sister every day. Oh, how I wish they could both see me now.

Trimming Hedges

Donnie was gone, Jim was gone, and I was at home on Trowbridge. In my life, all roads led back to Trowbridge, the home that had been in our family for what seemed like a hundred years. Sister was gone, and Terrye was away at college, but Mama was there. Me and Mama were the main coupleship.

At the start of the nineties, I was a forty-four-year-old woman still looking to get over in the one area where I knew I possessed unusual gifts—music. Because I had nurtured those gifts, they seemed to be strong and getting stronger every year. Because I worked out and kept in shape, I was ready to get in the ring the first chance I had. Trouble is, no promoters were interested.

Little things—*very* little things—came my way. I guess that's what they call the trickle-down effect. When I read that a show called *The Gospel Truth* was being produced in Detroit, I sprang into action. Mickey Stevenson, who had once been Clarence

Paul's partner and a Motown big shot, was writing and direct-ing. Mickey and I had little love for each other. But Mary Card, my Detroit friend who had worked on *Bubbling*, was one of the producers.

I called her to ask if she'd hire me.

"All we have left are understudies for the principals."

"I could be an understudy," I said.

"You'll be a lousy understudy. You're too self-assured to be under anything. You're a leading lady and nothing else."

"Agreed, but I need the money. Can I have the gig?"

"How can I turn down a friend?"

Mary didn't. She came through.

Jerome Shavers was the hairstylist for the show. We adored each other. Had it not been for Jerome, I would have gone crazy. Johnny Brown from *Good Times* was the star. Mickey Stevenson, who had devoted his life to becoming Berry Gordy, was in control of everyone and everything. He resented my presence. He knew I was far more experienced than the other women in the cast. He could order them around, but not me. He could impress them, but not me. That bothered him.

I knew I'd be working with true believers of the Baptist faith who'd never been in show business before. When I voiced my skepticism about religion, they said that everyone has to believe in something. So when I walked into the next rehearsal, I wore a T-shirt that expressed my solidarity. It read: "Everybody has to believe in something. I believe I'll roll another joint."

No wonder I was treated coldly. But sweet Jerome took care of me. I also instructed him in the fine art of wig design. He infuri-ated the cast by getting me my own table in the corner of the dressing room. He also secured a huge mirror. With my experience and his natural talent, we fashioned a fabulous hairdo for me, even though I was just one of the parishioners. They wouldn't give me a costume, so I created my own, a clingy gray silk dress. It was terribly sophisticated. That made the church ladies resent me even more.

"You don't look like you belong in church," said Mickey. "You look like you own the church."

Rehearsals went on. Jerome drove me a little crazy by playing his Jennifer Holliday records night and day. We opened to a lackluster reception. The girl I was understudying was weak and unconvincing. The rest of the cast knew that I could sing rings around her and would help the show enormously. But they were too busy with their prayer circles to speak up on my behalf. Mary was right. I was a lousy understudy.

Through Mary I learned that it was going to be a short run in Detroit. With my inside information, I gave the prayer-circle people a hard time.

"Does Jesus speak to you personally?" I asked one especially devout lady.

"Every day," she answered.

"Well, ask him how long this show's gonna run."

The lady didn't have the answer, but Mary did. A week before she gave the cast the word, she told me there would be only a few more performances.

Next time I walked by one of the prayer circles, I heard the Bible thumpers praying for the show to continue.

As I passed them, I whispered, "Pray all you like. The show's still gonna close."

When Mary found new financing and got the show to open in L.A., they wanted to drop me. But Mary came to my rescue again—no per diem, but I was kept on salary. Jerome set me up in an apartment and became my lifelong friend. He's still sending me gifts. When Jennifer Holliday joined the show, Jerome was especially excited. He adored her. I resented his fondness for Jennifer, and when I saw him accidentally drop her wig in a puddle of water, I couldn't help but howl.

Back in Detroit, what remained for me?

The good was very good. Back in 1985, Terrye had given birth to my first grandchild. I adored James and loved the role of Grandma. Marissa came along in 1991, making me even happier. Along with my daughter, they remain the lights of my life.

But grandkids, no matter how adorable and brilliant—and mine are both—could not make up for my broken-down career. I needed to be Bettye LaVette, and no matter how many times I had failed to do so before, I was still determined to try again.

Sometimes the afternoons were long. I kept myself sane by doing what Mama could no longer do—work in the yard. Trimming hedges can keep your arms fit. Smoking marijuana also added fuel to my already meticulous nature. I'd spend four, five hours cutting those bushes until they were so incredibly straight that folks driving by would stop, knock on my door, and ask for the name of my gardener.

Others gave me their cards, thinking I was the gardener. Humiliated, I'd go inside and take another toke. Other times someone might stop and say, "Didn't you used to be Bettye LaVette?" I'd nod, holding back the tears. In between drinks, I did a lot of crying. Other passersby were kinder. They simply complimented my garden and wanted to know where they

My mama, "Pretty Pearl" Haskins.

My daddy, Frank Haskins, and me, about six months old, outside the house in Muskegon.

Me at eighteen months.

662 Trowbridge,
where my career began.

With my daughter, Terrye Mathis,
when she was ten years old.

With my sister, Mattie,
around 1969.

Marrie Early,
the beauty to all,
at Sir John's in Miami, 1965.
(Courtesy Rene Hill)

Clarence Paul,
the greatest love,
the greatest scoundrel.

Me and my ponytail in 1963.

At Phelps Lounge
in Detroit, 1963.

At the Royal Peacock
in Atlanta, 1963.

Me and Jimmy Joy at the 20 Grand in Detroit, 1963.

With Gorgeous George, singer and tailor to the stars, at the Royal Peacock, 1963.

With the band at the Royal Peacock, 1965.

With singer Ted Taylor
at the Royal Peacock, 1965.

The Three: my driver and confidant Raymond Philpot, me, and Jim Lewis in 1968.

With my manager and mentor, Jim Lewis, 1972.

My first band, The Fun Company. Andrew Jones (drums), Don Hatcher (bass), Billy Hatcher (guitar), and Rudy Robinson (organ, musical director), circa 1968.

Betty LaVette 7½ copy Album

1 Do your duty – Also a Single
2 Loves made a fool out of me – B Side
3 Games people play
4 Made a woman out of me – Also a Single
5 Nearer to you – B Side
6 Easier to than do
7 Slip Around
8 Let me down Easy
9 Another Piece of my Heart
10 My Train's Comin' In – Single Only
11 I'm in Love
12 At the Mercy of a Man

Betty La Vette
662 Trowbridge
Detroit, Mich.
49202

The tape box of the
first debut album, which
was not released at the time,
circa 1970. The smudges
are from tears.

With Don Hatcher
(The Fun Company) in 1968.
I loved my miniskirts!

Cousin Margaret Nell
and Mama
in the "Blue Room"
on Trowbridge,
circa 1991.

With David Ruffin and Isaac Hayes, circa 1969.

With deejay Hal Jackson at Palisades Park, New Jersey, circa 1970.

Dressed as a 1920s character
in *Bubbling Brown Sugar,*
circa 1978.

With engineer Steve Melton at Muscle
Shoals Sound Studios in 1972, recording
the *second* debut album that was not
released at the time. *(Courtesy David Hood)*

At the Old Absinthe Bar in New Orleans, with Phil Parnell (keys)
and Jim Markway (bass) of my band Etcetera, 1981.

With Robert Hodge, my road manager, advisor, and friend for life, 1989.

Me and Margaret Nell, my oldest and dearest friend, in 2010.

With my second husband, Donnie Sadler, 1984.

On set, preparing for my weekly segment on
Barden Cablevision in Detroit, circa 1991.

With "Saint Frederick" Wilhelms III at
Sweetwater Music Hall in Mill Valley,
California, 2002.

With John Goddard,
the Crypt Keeper, in 2002.
*(Photo by Catherine Lyons-Labate.
Courtesy Village Music Archives)*

With Tom Gold, my personal agent, and Mike Kappus, president of the Rosebud Agency, in 2007.

Rehearsing a duet with Joe Henry and Mose Allison in Germany, 2008.

With Andrew Kaulkin, my guru, and president of the ANTI- record label, at Joe's Pub, 2005.

(Courtesy Julius "Juice" Freeman)

Me and
my husband,
Kevin Kiley,
in 2007.
(© Joseph A. Rosen)

Bonnie Raitt presenting me with the Rhythm & Blues
Foundation Pioneer Award, 2006.

(Courtesy Julius "Juice" Freeman)

Rehearsing with Drive-By Truckers'
Mike Cooley and Patterson Hood
at FAME Studios, 2007.

Jon Bon Jovi, me, and Rob Mathes
freezing and rehearsing in a tent for
Barack Obama's pre-inaugural
concert, 2009.

Me and Barack Obama, the first black president of
the United States of America, 2009.

Working out arrangements with Rob Mathes at Water Studios, Hoboken, 2011.

Me and my guys at the Café Carlyle, New York, 2012. Back row: Darryl Pierce (drums), Charles Bartels (bass), Brett Lucas (guitar), Alan Hill (keys, musical director). Front: Me and Robert Hodge (road manager).

With my granddaughter, Marissa Ross; my daughter, Terrye Mathis; and my grandson, Randall James Coats, 2011.

could go to hear me sing. The answer was the same. I was singing around town.

I was basically back to playing local bars. It was just me and my pianist, Rudy Robinson. We were booked into a little place on the Wayne State campus known as the Library. It didn't hold more than fifty customers. I liked the gig 'cause it was intimate and Rudy and I got to play whatever we liked. We might do a Beatles medley, or a Ray Charles medley, or even "St. James Infirmary." My repertoire was more eclectic than ever.

The Shadow Box, a nearby club, had closed down and their steady customers, looking for another perch, came to the Library. They were mainly a group of professional men in their fifties who liked to drink and listen to music. Most of them were married. They were engineers and supervisors, managerial types who had secure jobs with health insurance and pension plans. In this group was a distinguished gentleman named Robert Hodge, a tall and soft-spoken fan, who began to show up at the Library nearly every night.

I was friendly with all the customers, but especially with Robert, who asked about my history as a performer.

"I've been here and there," I said. "It's a long history."

"I don't mind listening," he said, "if you don't mind talking."

I never mind talking and I talked Robert's head off.

"Everyone calls me Bob," he said.

"You're too tall and impressive to be a Bob. You're a Robert. I'm calling you Robert."

Following my lead, all his friends started calling him Robert.

Robert had enjoyed a long, successful career in the high-level tech industry in Detroit. He was not especially warm and certainly not inclined to express his emotions. That was fine with me. I had enough emotional expressiveness for the both of us. Like me, he loved to drink. He was as good a drinking partner as I could ask for. Robert Hodge proved to be one of the best friends I'd ever had.

"Seems like you need to be playing bigger places than this," he said.

"The reality is I'm lucky to have this gig."

"Reality is a fluid thing. I see you upgrading."

"I've been trying to do just that for the past thirty years."

"You need help."

"I do," I said. "You willing?"

"I am."

"What kind of help you have in mind?" I asked.

"You tell me what kind you need."

"Money," I said. "Money is always appreciated."

"I can help you with that."

And he did. Robert Hodge, bless his heart, was the man who basically got me through the nineties.

Another man helped, though to a far lesser degree. His name was Ian Levine, and he showed up in Detroit sometime in the late eighties. He was an Englishman, an important fact because without the support of English fans, I might have disappeared entirely. Ian appeared as something of a savior, even if the savior happened to be a chubby groupie who was semi-famous for being the house deejay at Heaven, one of London's more glittery gay discos.

When I first met him, he said that he had come to Detroit to take up where Berry Gordy had left off.

"Berry closed down the party," he said. "Well, I'm starting it up all over again. And I'm calling it Motorcity Records."

He told me the story about how, when he was a young kid back in the sixties, he and his mom were on the same transatlantic flight as Berry Gordy and Diane Ross. He went up, introduced himself to them both, and was never the same. He went back to his seat and told Mom, "I'm going to be that man. I'm going to produce artists like Diane Ross."

Ian's dad, an owner of casinos in Great Britain, died, and with his inheritance from his father and his mother's permission, Ian took it upon himself to pick up the pieces of Motown and reclaim Gordy's empire. The problem, though, was plain: What was left of the empire—at least in Detroit—was in ruins.

Twenty years after Berry Gordy left his hometown, Ian Levine came from London to undo the damage. How can you not love a guy who has hatched this kind of crazy scheme? To understand where he was coming from, I had to understand the strange culture of the British movement called Northern Soul.

The Northern Soul nuts are hard-core R&B fans who respond to the funkier side of Motown. They pride themselves on loving the Detroit music and singers from the sixties who have gone unnoticed. The more obscure, the better. Since no one was more obscure than I was, I became a Northern Soul sweetheart. Among my early champions was David Godin, a writer who ran the record store Soul City in London and edited the magazine *Blues & Soul*. Godin discovered me before I discovered myself. He and other British writers like David Nathan never tired of singing my praises, even when the rest of the world didn't give a fuck.

Ian Levine was a product of this Northern Soul phenomenon. In addition to salvaging unheralded singers like me, Northern

Soul celebrated both pre- and post-disco grooves, giving them a highly synthesized electronic buzz. Beyond its nostalgia for hard-to-find, tough-minded R&B, Northern Soul was also about dance music. Deejays like Levine and others used a combination of old soul sounds and new frantic beats to keep the groove moving in certain London clubs.

When Levine arrived in Detroit, he had this kind of combination in mind. I'm hardly a purist, so it didn't bother me that he was using disco dance beats. Unlike most bullshit producers, Ian also came with cash in hand. He paid up front. He probably paid many of the old-time Motowners more than Berry Gordy ever had. He rounded up everyone, all the leftovers: Bobby Taylor, Marv Johnson, Kim Weston, Dennis Edwards, Eddie Kendricks, Brenda Holloway, the Contours, the Four Tops, the Marvelettes, the Velvelettes, even the Supremes (minus, of course, Miss Ross).

Some of the Motowners complained to Ian that I should not be included in his project. I was not an original Motowner. But Ian had championed me, as had many of the Northern Soul guys, and argued that *Tell Me a Lie*, my lone Motown album, legitimized me. Since Ian was paying, Ian got his way.

He had us gather on the lawn of the original Motown headquarters on West Grand and, standing right in front and waving his hands like a slightly crazed Cub Scout leader, posed as a photographer snapped the portrait. Motown rediscovered, Motown recaptured. It was all very surreal.

Ian found everyone, even the original Motown janitor, to participate in the project. Since most of us had little money, Ian gave us advances for clothes, makeup, and whatever else was needed. One of the singers was a lady from one of the original Motown female groups. Poor thing was strung out on crack. Beyond that, she had put on at least two hundred pounds since her glory days. On her way to the photography shoot, she stopped to get high with a couple of guys in a narrow alley wedged between two brick buildings. She squeezed into the alley okay, but after her hit of crack, she couldn't get out. Ian had to call an emergency unit to pry her loose. By the time the photographer took her picture, her wig was back on her head, and her lipstick straight, and her girdle in place.

The recordings—and there were dozens of them—were done at Sylvia Moy's studio in the huge home she bought with her royalties from "I Was Made to Love Her." You'll remember that, after Clarence Paul, Sylvia was a key creative force in Stevie Wonder's career. Ian gave Sylvia thousands of dollars to produce and engineer this enterprise. The records made no commercial or critical impact. In fact, most Motown fans hated Ian's productions. But I took the minority view. I liked the album he cut with me. I liked my version of "Jimmy Mack," and "I'm Ready for Love." I did them because Martha Reeves, who had sung with the Vandellas, refused to participate. She thought the Motorcity project was beneath her. I didn't. I liked the money. I liked redoing "Let Me Down Easy," Northern Soul style. I thought my cover of "Danger, Heartbreak Dead Ahead" was one of the funkiest things I'd ever done. Some people complained that the techno sound was synthesized and too slick. But to me, synthesizers are like vibrators. They may not be the real thing, but if you put them in the right place, they can do wonders.

I never expected or got royalties from Ian. But his upfront check didn't bounce and the record, issued and reissued under names like *Have a Heart* and *The Very Best of the Motorcity Record-ings*, hardly hurt my career—especially since, at that time, my career didn't exist.

The hustle never stops. When it does, you're either comatose or dead. Ian Levine helped my hustle. He was someone who had enough faith in me to let me record a whole album. No matter how bizarre or unsuccessful his efforts to revitalize the Detroit music scene were, his intentions were noble. He loved us and wanted to help us. Even more, it turned out that this Northern Soul passion for my singing style was real.

Twenty-five years after the Motown acts went to England to be greeted as heroes and heroines, I was invited over for a North-ern Soul Weekender—three days of concerts—in far-north Cleethorpes. It didn't matter that I hadn't heard of the city. It didn't matter that I was sharing the bill with Richard "Popcorn" Wylie whose early Motown group, Popcorn and the Mohawks, was even less known than I was. It didn't matter that Martha Reeves, a helluva lot more known than I was, was the star of the show. I was happy—on any terms, in any way—to get to Great Britain and see if I actually had fans over there. It turned out I did.

My entourage was small—me, Robert Hodge (by then my lover and manager), cousin Margaret, and Rudy Robinson. As long as Rudy was there, I could manage any music they might request. In those happy days before 9/11 when you could bring anything on the plane, Margaret brought a suitcase of mini bot-tles of Long Island iced tea. We partied all the way over. When we landed, I was so glad to be there I knelt down and kissed the ground. I looked up and saw people holding my 45s, wanting an autograph. That had never happened to me before. God bless England!

England was the first place I went where, in soul-music circles, everyone actually knew who I was. I didn't have to go through my usual explanation of "Well, I was first on Atlantic, and this happened and that happened . . ." The fans knew my history better than I did. My marginal status in America increased my status in England. The Brits considered themselves connoisseurs. They prided themselves in appreciating what Americans had neglected. In America, everyone knew about Etta James and Aretha Franklin, but most people had not heard of Bettye LaVette. That made Bettye LaVette even more attractive to the English, who were determined to lavish on her the attention she had so sorely missed.

I liked being lavished on. The more attention, the merrier. I was interviewed by writers who flattered me with intelligent questions. They had carefully studied my work. Not only were they sympathetic to my buzzard-luck career, they were loving. So were the crowds at the show. I felt like a star.

And then it was time to go back home.

Back to High School

I t sounds ridiculous. It was ridiculous. But I was in Detroit—trapped in Detroit, jobless in Detroit, homebound in Detroit—and I needed to do something to stave off boredom, not to mention insanity.

I had gone to Northern High School for a brief time. It was not far from my house and I passed by it practically every day. I'd see the Northern High girls walk down the street, sloppily dressed, combs in their hair, looking like boys, and I'd think, *Lord, what have these children come to!*

For all my wild days and nights, I never let my appearance deteriorate, not for a minute. I hated to see this next generation of young girls be so indifferent about their looks. When I stepped out into the world, I did so with confidence because my speech, dress, posture, and whole demeanor were those of a proud woman.

I knew that Northern High had a summer program. I also

knew some of the people who ran it. They remembered me from my days at the Graystone Ballroom and the 20 Grand. I spoke to one about letting me run a mentoring program for young girls. Just like that, I was hired. That meant a weekly paycheck from the city as well as a chance to teach something I felt strongly about—good grooming. On the first day of class, I was filled with enthusiasm and righteous purpose.

I arrived in the gym where a dozen girls were waiting for me. One of them was seated on a stool. She was slouched down over her boyfriend, who had his head between her legs. She was braiding his hair, scratching off his dandruff, and acting like this was the most natural thing in the world.

"I came here today," I said, "to talk about what it means to be demure. Do you have any idea what that means?"

The girl doing the braiding didn't even look up.

"I'm talking to you," I said. "What does 'demure' mean?"

"Got no idea."

"Well, it's certainly not what you're doing now. Do you have any idea how awful you look? You're braiding his hair while your own hair looks like it got caught in a blender."

Still no answer.

Finally, I walked over, looked her in the eye, and said, "You look like a slovenly bitch."

Next day her mother came to school and said, "Did you call my daughter a slovenly bitch?"

"Those were my exact words."

"You got no right to say that."

I looked at her mother and was about to say, *You're even more of a slovenly bitch than she is,* but I held my tongue. Instead, I said, "We all have the right to tell the truth."

"You hurt her feelings."

"If that's what it takes to get her to face reality, I'm glad."

"With that mouth of yours," said the mother, "you shouldn't be teaching here."

"I'm not a teacher. I'm a rhythm-and-blues singer trying to help these girls. I've been all over the world, and if they listen to me, they just might learn something."

"You still don't got no business being here."

The mother was right, even if it took me another month to admit it.

As a teacher, I tried, but I got nowhere.

"When you're waiting for a bus," I told the girls, "and you got a cigarette dangling out of your mouth and you're chewing gum like a cow and you're wearing short shorts riding up the crack of your ass, what do you think you look like?"

"Who cares," said one of the girls.

"What business is it of yours?" asked another.

These girls were impossible. Nothing I said made even the slightest impression. Every night I'd call up Robert Hodge, then my main man, and say, "Why am I fooling with these bitches when they couldn't care less about how they look?"

"Good question. What's the answer?"

"I got nothing else to do."

"We can get some more flyers out. We can send out more of your CDs."

God bless Robert. When the world had given up on me, he hadn't. He put his money where his mouth was. He worked tirelessly to promote me to an uninterested music industry. He'd put together sample CDs of tracks from old records, he'd write bios and press releases, he'd send out mailings to record companies, big and little, all over the country. When I needed a car, he'd buy me one. When I needed a good meal, he'd take me to a fancy restaurant. When I needed a shoulder to cry on, he was always there.

One of those times I needed to cry most was during the summer of 1991 when I got word that my friend David Ruffin had died in a Philadelphia crack house. David and Marvin were two of the best singers to come out of Motown. I knew them back at a time when the crack pipe—apparently a cause in both their downfalls—had not yet swept through the neighborhood. I knew them at a time when they were still clear and creative, artists operating on the highest level imaginable. These were beautiful men with beautiful poetry in their souls. Then in 1992, Eddie Kendricks, Ruffin's fellow Temptation, died in his hometown of Birmingham, Alabama.

Why some of us who drank heavily, smoked weed continually, and blew cocaine did not submit to the pipe while others did remains a mystery. In my case, maybe I sensed its deadly property. Just as I had seen how heroin could make me nod out like Esther Phillips, I saw how the pipe could do the same. I've never been afraid of experimenting with sex or drugs, but I have been afraid of falling apart physically. That fear has kept me away from the pipe. Maybe it's my vanity or my common sense. Whatever it is, it's kept me alive.

My active role in the political life of Detroit also helped. That was part of Jim Lewis's legacy. He had introduced me to many of the city's leaders and arranged my appointment to several boards, including the ones overseeing the public library and city zoo. These led to my performing at formal functions. I was also an active Democrat and supporter of Mayor Coleman Young, a friend, from the outset of his political career. I sang at dozens of the mayor's events during his nineteen years in office. Because I knew many members of the Board of Education and some of the higher-ups in the police department, I was often called to perform at fund-raising dinners. My friends in local government helped see me through.

In 1992, I surprised myself by getting involved in presidential politics. I was one of the earliest and strongest backers of Ross Perot. In fact, I was the first black in Michigan to volunteer in his campaign. My boyfriend/manager Robert was working for Electronic Data Systems, the company Perot founded, and had good things to say about him. He showed me videos of his speeches. I liked what Perot had to say. I liked his independence. He was pro-choice and took a bold stance in advocating an Environmental Protection Agency. Black-centric candidates like Jesse Jackson did not appeal to me. (His status as a preacher lessened that appeal even more.) I also took the position that we weren't looking to elect a president of black America, but of all America. I didn't trust Clinton and couldn't stomach old man Bush. There was a moment when Perot's campaign caught fire and, as assistant to the president of his Michigan chapter, I liked being on the front lines. His loss was disappointing but not unexpected. I felt good about backing someone with integrity.

I have a knack for staying organized. I'm almost obsessively efficient as a gardener and housekeeper. Those qualities aided my ability to get through the lean years without losing my mind. So did my drive to get back in the limelight, even on a local level. I became a big fish in a small pond.

Because everyone from the black radio stations knew me from the sixties, I was well connected with the media. One of those connections led to my hosting a Christmas special on local cable

TV. I wore a red velvet gown and, like Loretta Young, made a sweeping entrance walking down a long spiral staircase as I sang "The Christmas Song." I had the Contours, one of the original Motown groups, on the show as well as my grandkids and cousin Margaret's nephews and nieces. For a short while, I had my own afternoon TV show where I interviewed entertainers and politicians. I thought all this exposure might help me get a record deal.

But who was I fooling? Detroit looked like Dresden after World War II. There was absolutely nothing happening. The nineties were rough. Celebrating my fiftieth birthday, I was happy to be alive and kicking, happy to be in shape. I hadn't gained weight and was basically the same dress size I was in high school. I was happy to have my voice sounding as strong as ever. I was happy to have a man like Robert Hodge devoted to my well-being and willing to give me whatever I needed. I was happy to have him looking after my career.

But what career?

The same local clubs, the same local political dinners, the same local radio or TV appearances. After fifty years, I was still stuck in Dodge.

Cousin Margaret was a constant comfort and so was Mama. Never once did my mother even hint that I should give up on show business. She watched me live my life in an extremely unorthodox manner and yet never passed judgment.

"You can sing, baby," she'd say, "and you got to keep trying. You know what's happened in the past, but you don't know the future. Your future looks bright to me."

At ninety-one, she was going strong. Her only problem was arthritis. But that didn't stop her from drinking. She drank in a peculiar way. She kept a glass on the kitchen counter and poured a shot of vodka. Then she walked out of the kitchen, did some little housecleaning chore, and fifteen minutes later came back and took a sip of vodka along with a sip of water. The pattern continued all day long. It was hard to tell just how many glasses of vodka she downed by the time she went to bed, but it was more than a few. Never a fall-down drunk, she was often tipsy. I was hardly in a position to criticize her behavior. First of all, she was ninety-one, and no matter how you looked at it, she had beaten the odds. And second, as a drinker and marijuana smoker myself, who was I to pass judgment?

The truth, though, is that booze caused her to fall. She was wobbly when she reached out for her great-granddaughter Marissa, lost her footing, and landed on the floor.

"Something's wrong," she said. "I can't get up."

"Don't try, Mama. I'm calling nine-one-one."

After she was examined in the hospital, the diagnosis came quickly. She'd broken her hip.

"I'm dying," she said, in her typical dramatic fashion.

"No, you're not, Mama. You just broke your hip."

The next day she came out of surgery with a good report from the doctor.

"It went flawlessly," he said. "However, I have to tell you that even with successful surgery most people her age don't survive very long. The operation itself takes a terrible toll on the body."

"Mama's different," I assured him.

"She has to give up her snuff and her vodka."

"Did you tell her that?"

"I did."

"And what'd she say?" I asked.

"She laughed at me like I was crazy."

"That's Mama."

"And she also has to stay put. Keep her from getting up and moving around."

"That's like telling the sun not to rise."

"You must try."

I did, and I failed, and two weeks later Mama was dead.

We buried this good woman, this crazy but absolutely devoted mother, this lady who gave me my tenacity and spirit of survival.

There are mystics who say we choose our own parents, intuitively knowing what we need to survive this mean ol' world. If that's true, I picked the right people, a father who adored me unreservedly and a mother who stuck with me through thick and thin. Their love was the powerful nourishment I needed—and still draw on—to do what I have to do.

Marrie Early had come to live in Detroit. Her children and many relatives were there. Her presence brought great comfort to me because her spirit was so unique and absolutely positive, no matter how complicated her love life.

Every time we spoke, which was often, she had an encouraging word for me.

"I know you're going to be a bigger star than all of them," she'd say, when I had gone through an especially tough week.

"How can you say that," I asked, "when last night I was singing at a club in front of three people—and that includes the bartender?"

"But I bet those three people loved every note you sang."

"You aren't gonna let me get depressed, are you, Marrie?"

"Not with your voice. Not with your talent. You ain't got no reason to be depressed. You got everything to live for."

"So do you, baby. You've got to be the most loved woman in all the world."

Marrie laughed off my compliment, but I meant it with all my heart. Next time I heard from her, the cheerfulness was still in her voice, in spite of the worst possible news.

"I guess you better come over here and visit me, Bettye," she said, "or there won't be anyone here to visit."

"What are you talking about, Marrie?"

"They tell me I got cancer."

I couldn't say a word. I had to catch my breath. "I'm coming over right now."

The last days of Marrie Early were unforgettable. She was in a hospital bed in her living room where, despite her disease, she appeared healthy and gorgeous. Her house was always filled with friends, neighbors, and children. It felt more like a party than a death watch. In attendance were also many of the men who had been her lovers. None of them were angry or jealous of one another. They were there simply because they adored Marrie. The most remarkable thing, though, was Marrie's attitude. She was so cool with dying that she made us all comfortable. I held back my tears, yet none of those men could. They were crying like babies, while Marrie was comforting them. Because she had been a nurse, she was doing most of the caretaking.

"It ain't no thing," she said.

"Ain't no thing! Marrie, I can't even think about what this world is going to be like without you."

"It's gonna be fine. Gonna be a world where Bettye LaVette will be seen as the best singer there is."

A record by Yanni, the New Age musician, was playing on the phonograph. I couldn't stand it.

"I don't want you dying with this music playing," I said. "You deserve something better than this."

"It keeps me calm. It's what I want," she said.

There was no arguing. Marrie Early was orchestrating her final days and doing a beautiful job. She had me make her gumbo. She had her table set with her best sterling silver and Wedgwood. She had her children seated on a lovely silk turquoise chaise longue so she could take pride in their appearance. They in turn had made a collage of photographs of Marrie with all her famous friends—Sam Cooke, Brook Benton, the Midnighters, Little Willie John, Redd Foxx, Jeffrey Osborne. There was a blowup of a picture of her in a bikini that looked like it was sewn with shoestrings.

This lady who was as sexually free as anyone somehow found a way not to alienate anyone, not even the men she had been with. Every last one of them not only still loved her, but was willing to honor her as she breathed her last breath.

In a world where human beings are the most messed-up creatures of all, Marrie Early was a miracle.

A Woman Like Me

In 1999, as people starting talking about the start of a new millennium, I could hardly get excited. I had a distinct feeling that the new millennium would bear a striking resemblance to the old one. If I hadn't made it in my twenties, thirties, or forties, what were the chances of making it in my fifties? Cold-blooded objectivity said not so good. Hope and optimism said keep on keeping on. Fortunately, hope and optimism won out.

I was still hustling for work, still local as local can be. As much as I love Detroit and as proud as I am of our rich musical heritage, I was stuck in a city of broken dreams and faded glory.

Then the phone rang.

"Bettye LaVette?"

"Speaking."

"My name's Randall Grass, and you don't know me."

"I sure don't."

"I run a record label."

"Well, then I want to know you."

"I've been a fan of yours for years."

"What's the name of your label?"

"Shanachie Records."

"And you want to record me?"

"Wish I could. I'm afraid I'll never get the approval of my board."

"Then why the fuck are you calling me?"

"I just wanted to tell you . . ."

"Listen, mister, I appreciate my fans, no matter how few they may be. And if you're a fan, I appreciate you. But to get me on the phone to say that number one, you're a fan, and number two, you have a record label, but number three, you can't record me . . . well, that seems like an exercise in cruelty."

"I didn't mean to be cruel, only honest," said Grass. "I honestly feel you're a great singer, but Shanachie is extremely concerned about the commercial potential of each artist. We have super-tight budgets, and I'd have a hard time arguing that your record would sell."

"I'm not interested in any arguments. I just want another record out, and if you can help to that end, then we have something to talk about."

"I think I can."

"How?"

"I'm going to find you a booking agency, a record deal, or a gig."

"Beautiful," I said.

"It just might take a while."

"I'm not going anywhere."

Yet in truth, I was. As the millennium ended and America remained indifferent to Bettye LaVette, Europe was starting to show real interest. I was gigging at blues festivals in France, Italy, and Germany. I played the Blues Estafette in Utrecht, Holland, where Munich Records producer Ben Mattijssen saw my performance. He was so impressed that later he recorded a concert and did a TV special with me and Rudy. *Let Me Down Easy: In Concert* became my first live album.

I was rummaging through my attic when I came across a box marked "LaVette Sessions." Inside was a tape. When I went to a local studio to hear it, my hope was confirmed. It was the unreleased album that I did with Brad Shapiro back in 1972 for Atlantic's Atco subsidiary. Due to a big warehouse fire that had destroyed hundreds of Atlantic masters, most collectors had presumed my record had gone up in flames. Yet here it was! It wasn't the master, but it sounded great. Because I had almost no proof of my existence during my long down years, I kept these reel-to-reel tapes close to my heart. They were proof that I had done something.

After my friend Paul Williams at Sony transferred my reel-to-reel to cassette, I sent it to my friend Gilles Petard, whom I had met in Grace Jones's dressing room during the disco era. Gilles had long championed my music.

Gilles called me on the very day he received the music.

"*C'est magnifique!*" he cried.

"Magnificent enough to put out?" I asked.

"Are you kidding, Bettye? Is the *Mona Lisa* magnificent enough to hang in the Louvre? I'll arrange for a European release of this material—and I'll do it this year."

Gilles flew to America, searched the Atlantic vault, found the master, and put it out.

Suddenly, with two European releases in 2000, the European soul magazines gave me more publicity than I had received in years. I won't say I was hot, but I was certainly lukewarm.

Back to square one.

I was back to trimming hedges.

Robert Hodge stayed steady. He kept sending press materials to anyone with the slightest connection to a label.

My old friend Mack Rice had been working with producer Jon Tiven, who had produced Wilson Pickett. Mack said that Tiven had contacts with big labels and was interested in me. Was I interested in him? I was—mainly because no one else was calling.

When word got around that I was considering going into the studio with Tiven, I got an e-mail from someone I'd never met.

Dear Bettye,

Hope you don't mind if I call you by your first name, but I've been listening to your records for years and consider you the best singer out there. I'm writing not only to tell you how much I admire you, but to say that I hope the news I recently read on the Southern Soul website isn't true. There was a post saying that you're going to be produced by Jon Tiven. I think that's a mistake and hope you'll reconsider.

The e-mail ticked me off, and I found myself responding immediately.

Listen, muthafucka, who are you to tell me what producer to use? Are you a producer? Do you have money to buy me studio time? Do you have any fuckin' idea how hard it is to get a deal?

He wrote back.

I understand why you'd be pissed. I didn't mean any disrespect, only that your talent is so great it requires the best production. I just don't think Tiven is right for the job. I'm not a producer. I'm a fan—probably your biggest fan. And I just want you to do great.

I wrote back, "Who appointed you the overseer of my career?"
He wrote back, "No one. But you'll never find anyone who loves your singing as much I do."
"What do you do for a living?" I asked.
"Buy and sell antiques."
"I love antiques. I'm somewhat of an antique myself."
The e-mails flew back and forth, and got me curious about my new highly opinionated pen pal. His name was Kevin Kiley, and our paths were about to converge.

Still looking for a deal?" asked Randall Grass, the Shanachie label exec who proved to be a good friend.
"Hell, yes."
"Got an idea."
"Shoot."
"Ever hear of Dennis Walker?"

"No."

"Ever hear of Robert Cray?"

"I think so. Young blues guy?"

"That's him. Ever hear his 'Right Next Door'?"

"Yes, I like it."

"Well, it was written by Cray and Dennis Walker. Walker produced it. He's won Grammys. I think he's the perfect producer and writer for you."

"What does *he* think?"

"He thinks it's a good fit. He's looking for a female singer. Better yet, he's got a deal on a label called Blues Express. They've hired him to write and produce a whole record—and they're letting him pick the vocalist."

"Tell him to call me."

A half-hour later, he did.

An hour into our conversation—I was in Detroit, Dennis in Burbank—we were drawn to each other. Over a period of time, the attraction grew stronger.

The challenge, of course, was Robert. When he came into my life, I had other suitors, but I found him the most suitable. He gave me everything I wanted and, in return, made me promise I wouldn't fuck around on him. I had kept the promise, but now things were changing.

When I got the parcel of songs that Dennis Walker sent, I saw that he was a white man who understood rhythm-and-blues as deeply as the blackest black. I liked about eighty percent of everything he wrote, and I liked a hundred percent of what he was telling me on the phone. He was seductive in all ways: He told me that he loved my voice—a compliment guaranteed to win me over—and that he knew just how to make me happy in the studio.

He was a poet who spoke beautifully. When he sent me his material, I loved the lyrics. Even though all of them had not been written specifically for me, they all felt that way. From Dennis's perspective, my voice was perfect for his songs. He kept saying that he was falling for me.

When I got to California to cut the record, Dennis and I connected on every level, as though we'd known each other our entire lives. The relationship took me all the way back to the sixties, where the producer/writer was also your mentor/lover. Everything was great—his fabulous house jutting out from the side of a mountain with a world-class view, his appreciation of what I could do vocally, his vision for what I knew was going to be nothing less than a sensational rhythm-and-blues album, the purest R&B album of my career. There was only one tiny problem.

Before the project began, Dennis had been arrested for drug conspiracy and was out on bail.

"No matter," he said. "We'll get the thing recorded before my case comes up."

"If you say so, baby," I said, eager to get my voice on these funky tracks.

When it came to personnel, though, Dennis and I clashed.

"I want to bring in the Memphis Horns," he said.

"The Memphis Horns are great," I said, "but every damn time they've played on one of my records, the record has flopped. I've had enough of the Memphis Horns."

So Dennis brought in the horns from *The Tonight Show* band. I always loved their sound. All I needed was Rudy Robinson.

"I don't think he's right for this record," said Dennis.

"You're crazy," I said. "He's the best musician I know. I've fought with him for thirty-five years, but I won't record without him. No one knows me like Rudy. No one has his finesse or funk. No Rudy, no me."

"I'll give you Rudy, but you gotta give me the cats I've been using for the Robert Cray records."

"Long as they understand that they gotta follow Rudy wherever he goes. Rudy's direction is my direction."

"You really like your piano player, don't you?"

"I don't use the word 'genius' very often, but that's what Rudy is."

Rudy came to L.A., and so did Cray's sidemen. The sessions were fiery. The songs caught my spirit and had me singing harder and smarter than I'd ever sung. They had an edge of intelligence that much of R&B lacks. I left Burbank convinced I'd cut a near-perfect rhythm-and-blues record.

When they sent me the final mix, though, I was horrified to hear how dominant Dennis had made the organ. Organs remind me of funerals. Rather than argue with him, I got Robert Hodge to buy me a plane ticket and flew back out to Burbank where I got the goddamn organ off the record. The next day he was hauled off to jail. I got the record I wanted.

Happy ending?

Not yet.

Another instance of sugar turning to shit?

Afraid so.

More buzzard luck?

Hell, yes.

The head of the record company disappeared. No one knew where to find him or what would happen to the masters. So I had no choice but to go get those tapes and bring them back to

Detroit. One way or another, the album had to come out. After a countless number of false starts and agonizing delays, it was finally released in 2003 on the Blues Express label, but I never saw a dime of royalties. At least I had a record out there that showcased the present-tense power of my voice.

A sad footnote to this project: Not long after we got through recording, Rudy died. I dedicated *A Woman Like Me* to his memory, calling him "my friend, my left tonsil, and my music director." Like Jim Lewis, Rudy Robinson helped forge my soul as a singer. He completed me. He led me and followed me. He heard in me what I didn't hear in myself. He was crazy for sure, but no crazier than I was. And together, these two crazies made musical sense. I miss him like crazy.

The Dennis Walker record was another one of those triumphant debacles that characterize my career. The music was great, but no one really heard it. It lived—and still does—on the margins of the mainstream audience.

I kept looking for the right record deal. I thought I had a good lead with Scott Billington, who produced for Rounder Records and worked with Irma Thomas. His sound was a little clean for me, but I knew I could make it nastier. Billington expressed all sorts of enthusiasm but never came through.

For all these frustrations, though, I felt something shifting. The biggest shift of all happened in the smallest way, by my singing a couple of songs at a birthday party.

Rosebud and ANTI-

In 1941, five years before I was born, *Citizen Kane*, directed by and starring Orson Welles, was released. The life story of a character based on newspaper mogul William Randolph Hearst, the movie opens with Kane's final word before dying: "Rosebud." It then takes the entire film to explain what "Rosebud" means.

I was in my mid-fifties before I understood what Rosebud meant to me. It was the name of the booking agency that finally took me from the minor to the major leagues.

Mike Kappus ran the Rosebud Agency. They booked big acts, including Robert Cray. I wanted and needed an outfit like Rosebud. Before he went to jail, Dennis Walker had urged me to contact Kappus. I wasn't shy about contacting anyone. I sent Mike a copy of *A Woman Like Me*.

"The album's great," said Mike, when I finally got him on the phone. "It's one of the best R&B records I've ever heard."

"So you'll book me?"

"I can't."

"Why?"

"You have no real management. You have no real record label."

"But I'm real," I said. "Hell, I'm as real as it gets."

"Sorry, Bettye. But I do wish you the best."

Only a few weeks later, I got a call from John Goddard, owner of Village Music in Mill Valley. John is another one of those angelic music lovers who spends his time helping long-suffering artists get their due. He was a key force behind the comeback of Little Jimmy Scott.

"I'd love for you to sing at my birthday party," he said. "I'm having a two-night celebration."

As he went over the guest list—Bonnie Raitt, Steve Miller, Huey Lewis—I took special note when he mentioned Mike Kappus.

For years, people had been saying that hearing my records was one thing, but hearing and seeing me live was a whole different experience. I wanted Kappus to see me live.

Goddard's parties made the difference. After Michael saw my show, he did a complete turnaround, saying that he wanted to book me. I was off and running.

Learning to navigate the Internet also made a difference. I saw that I had fans and friends in places I'd never imagined. One was Frederick Wilhelms III, another angel, this one disguised as a lawyer. We called him Saint Frederick because he was on a god-like mission to find royalties for artists who'd been screwed out of money. Saint Frederick took me on, and while he didn't find me a fortune, he did uncover payments and got checks coming my way. He did me all sorts of favors and charged me practically nothing.

In a field where entertainment lawyers are justifiably maligned, he was nothing short of magnificent.

Things were turning around. The big break with Rosebud meant I could work—and Mike Kappus kept me working all the time. I'd never been happier. I was built for a busy career and, despite middle age—or maybe because of middle age—I was able to handle it. I didn't have any distractions. I didn't harbor any doubts. Work was what I wanted.

I started working bigger festivals like crazy, and for the first time in decades, I was actually making a living. To be on a bill, in America or Europe, with Etta James and Bobby Bland was an honor. My billing as a traditional blues singer didn't thrill me, but I was thrilled to win a W. C. Handy Award from the Blues Foundation in Memphis for Comeback Blues Album of the Year— *A Woman Like Me.* Even though it was an R&B record, who was I to quibble with categories? Besides, even during the purest of the blues festivals, I did just what Jim Lewis had taught me to do. I sang anything I wanted to.

My correspondence with Kevin Kiley had gone from e-mails to phone calls. I had started a flirtation and wasn't thrilled when he sent me a Christmas card with a picture of him and his girlfriend. I didn't want him to like anyone but me. After a while, he exposed his hand; he said he was falling for me. He was a genuine person, and I realized that I needed to respond to his genuineness. I also realized that he was a far better person than I was. It was a compliment that someone so good would be attracted to me. So when he said he was coming to an antiques show in Detroit and wanted to take me to dinner, I readily accepted.

When he showed up at the house and saw me for the first time, he said, "You're little."

Proud that I'd never lost my figure, I took that as a compliment.

"Careful," I said, as he walked down the steps to my blue basement, "that's where Stevie Wonder bumped his head."

On the way to dinner, I played him *A Woman Like Me* in the car. He liked it, but he wasn't shy about critiquing it.

"You're ready to critique everything, aren't you?" I asked.

"I love your singing," he said, "but I have to be honest about the production."

Honesty turned out to be one of Kevin's chief qualities. The other was generosity. That night he gave me an exquisitely custom-designed multi-CD package of my complete recorded work. He even commissioned John Ridley to write liner notes. No one had ever bothered to do this before. It was the most precious and loving gift I have ever received. I couldn't help but cry.

We had a great time, and at the end of our first date, he leaned over and kissed me.

"My fans don't kiss me," I said.

"This one does."

Kevin Kiley turned out to be a helluva guy. He had all the right attributes—bright, handsome, sexy, and younger than I was. It didn't hurt that he knew everything about me. Fact is, when it came to soul music, he was a serious scholar. We loved each other's company. I felt love was coming my way. The problem, though, was Robert Hodge. I take that back. Robert was never a problem. He was—and remains—a blessing in my life. Robert was Mr. Loyalty, a man, like Jim Lewis, who had stuck by me through thick and thin. He was also my boyfriend and someone who insisted that, when it came to lovers, there could be no others. I tried to stay faithful and did—until Dennis Walker came along. Once Dennis was gone, I was back walking the straight and narrow. But this Kevin Kiley was something else. Not only was he down-to-earth and refreshingly candid in all his opinions, he was a good singer—a white guy with a black style— who gigged in local bars around northern New Jersey. Kevin was more talented than I was. He could play many instruments, while I could play none.

When I went to West Orange and visited his home, I saw his beautiful antiques and his amazing vinyl collection. He was a neat freak like I was. His pretty two-story house, situated on a quiet tree-lined street, had a big backyard with all sorts of green- ery. By then, Kevin and I were getting closer and closer. Musi- cally, culturally, and—you guessed it—sexually, we were a perfect pair. Our only roadblock was Robert.

Other women have asked me, "Bettye, you've had all these men. You've gone from one to another and yet I don't see any of them angry at you. How do you do it?"

I don't know. I've been lucky and I've also been choosy. Aside from my first husband, the evil pimp who nearly killed me, and someone like Gene Chandler, I've gravitated toward men who've understood and accepted me for who I am. Of all those men, Robert Hodge turned out to be the most loving and gracious. He wasn't happy when I told him that I had fallen for Kevin, but his devotion was so great that he stayed on to be part of my manage- ment team. His care for me overwhelmed his romantic attach- ment. Today, Robert remains my constant companion on the road. As if that weren't enough, he and Kevin have become close friends. For that I'm extremely grateful.

My relationship with Kevin was intense. We met in October of 2002 and were married in July of 2003. At age fifty-seven, I became a blushing bride.

How lucky can one girl be?

Luck had never seemed to go my way, and I'm not sure it was luck that turned the tables. I'd credit the change to pure tenacity. I was simply too headstrong to quit. After all I had been through, after everything Jim Lewis had taught me, after a lifetime of experience, I knew goddamn well I could sing—and I wasn't about to go away quietly.

Eager to get me connected to a label, Mike Kappus introduced me to Ry Cooder. I hadn't heard of him, but Kevin had. Kevin was excited that the producer of *Buena Vista Social Club* wanted to produce me. We got together with Ry who was enthusiastic about working with me. He said he'd been in three different bands that had played versions of "He Made a Woman Outta Me." He had connections with major labels. I saw myself at Warner or RCA, Sony or Universal. It turned out, though, that Ry's high-priced producer fee, along with my weak sales history, created an unacceptable package. All the majors passed.

Mike had another idea. After one of my shows, he came to my dressing room with this tall, white, hippie-looking dude with a big Afro, a dirty T-shirt, no socks, and a sweet smile.

"This is Andrew Kaulkin of ANTI-," said Mike.

"Hi, Andrew," I said. "What's an ANTI-?"

"My record label."

"Wish I had heard of it."

"That's okay, I've heard of you—and I love you. Loved the show. Would love to record you."

"Just like that?"

"Well, we'll have to talk about material and producers, but I want you on my label."

My first thought was, *I need a record so bad and this is what I was sent? I need a major label, not a guy with a big Afro and no socks.*

"We may not be a major label," said Andrew, reading my mind, "but we're proud and aggressive and completely independent."

"Sounds like me," I said.

"I was hoping you'd say that."

Andrew turned out to be another angel. It took me awhile to adjust to the idea of a label run by young people, but those young people won me over. After more than a half-century in the business, this was the first time I felt like I had the long-term support of a record company that saw my artistic potential.

Andrew Kaulkin had dozens of ideas. That's why I started calling him my musical guru. But being one of those people who must challenge gurus, even my own, I naturally challenged Andy when he suggested an album of songs written by women.

"I'm not sitting around for hours and listening to a bunch of girls sing," I said. "Aside from a couple of good relationships, I've never gotten along with girls all that well. When it comes to other women, I'm more competitive than friendly."

"Trust me, Bettye," said Andy. "We'll find songs you can sink your teeth into—songs written from a woman's point of view."

Andy brought in Joe Henry, a producer who had won a Grammy for a CD he had recently done with Solomon Burke. Like Ry, Joe was eager. He praised me to the sky. He said he couldn't wait to work with me in the studio. Great. Let's get started.

But then word came down that Joe had gone in a different

direction and didn't have time for me. I suddenly saw that old pattern again. Was this a reemergence of my buzzard luck? Another instance of my finding the right musical companion only to have the companion disappear? I couldn't help but worry.

Thankfully, Joe reconsidered and came on board. He wanted to produce me after all. So Joe, Andy, and Kevin, with his encyclopedic knowledge of music, went to work. They must have come up with a hundred tunes before we picked ten. None of them were R&B vehicles. Because I felt I had mastered the R&B song—nothing would ever outdo *A Woman Like Me*—I wanted to be challenged by other genres. For instance, I've always loved country. I adored Bobbie Cryner's "Just Say So." In figuring out Dolly Parton's "Little Sparrow," a real heartbreaker, I felt the lyrics were too wordy for me. I took lines like "Oh, but I'm not a sparrow" and cut them to "I ain't no sparrow." In rendering rock songs, I also had to find myself in the stories. Lucinda Williams's "Joy" took on a slightly different lyrical form. Lucinda implied that she was looking for love; I was looking for Bettye LaVette. Later, by the way, I got to meet Lucinda, whom I liked immensely. (She's also one of the few women who can possibly outdrink me.) Songs by Joan Armatrading and Aimee Mann became highly personal statements for me. And in one case—Sinéad O'Connor's "I Do Not Want What I Have Not Got"—the lyrics became a statement of what I saw as a new chapter in my life. To this day, it's the encore to all my shows; it's become my anthem.

I'm walking through the desert
and I'm not scared though it's so hot
I have everything that I've ever requested
and I do not want what I have not got

I have learned so many things from my mother
Oh, see how happy she has made me
I will take this road so much further
Though I know not where it takes me

I have water for my journey
I have bread and I've got my wine
No longer will I be hungry
For the bread of life is mine

I'm walking through the desert
and I'm not scared though it's so hot
I have everything that I've ever requested
and I do not want what I have not got

I've Got My Own Hell to Raise got great reviews and sold more copies than anything I had previously done. Andy and his ANTI-band of tattooed elves established me as a serious artist. Joe Henry produced the record tastefully without diluting the funk. There was a story line that ran through the album. It was the story of a woman who had suffered but survived. The sparrow could still fly. Joy was possible. I could truthfully say, "I do not want what I have not got." I could claim victory.

I also saw that, even though there wasn't a single traditional R&B song on the album, this suite of songs was shot through with soul. Because I had to search, and sometimes struggle, to find the meanings, I went deeper than I had gone before.

I was also sure I had a chance for a Grammy. But the fates were against me. A clerk at ANTI- forgot to submit it. Bonnie Raitt tried to rectify the situation; she and other Grammy winners asked that the deadline be extended so I might be considered, but no such luck.

I did, however, get to sing "Little Sparrow" on David Letterman's show. The next day I got a call from Steve Buckingham, my former producer who had collaborated with Dolly Parton, the composer of the song.

"You were beautiful, Bettye," he said. "Just as beautiful as ever. I'm glad your career is taking off."

I wanted to say, *Where were you when my career was in the toilet and you were too busy working with Dolly to answer my calls, muthafucka?* But I decided to hold my tongue.

"Thank you, Steve," was all I said.

My personal life had changed as dramatically as my professional life. I moved from Detroit to the lovely home Kevin and I share in West Orange. The move made my dear cousin Margaret absolutely furious. She didn't speak to me for a year. I could understand her anger. She felt like I was deserting her—my best friend—as well as the city that I loved so well. There was no arguing with those facts. But there was also no denying the truth— that life looked brighter in a prosperous bedroom community in northern New Jersey than in forlorn Detroit.

In 2007, Donnie Sadler's mother called to say that he had passed. Kevin and I went to Philadelphia for the funeral. His demise had been slow and devastating. He was down to skin and bones. I sat in church and thought about that period in my life when Donnie had represented the hope of a future that never materialized for either of us. Death at an early age, especially for a man as sweet as Donnie, is inconsolably tragic.

The next day, tragedy was on my mind as I flew to Nashville

to record, ironically enough, my version of Bruce Springsteen's "Streets of Philadelphia." It was written about AIDS for the movie *Philadelphia*, and while I had many dear friends who were struck down by that disease, I was thinking of Donnie's battle with MS when I sang about how he'd been bruised and battered, how his legs felt like stone, and how he was unable to recognize himself in the mirror.

My interpretation was included in *Song of America*, a three-CD selection of seminal compositions that tell the history of the country, collected by, of all people, music fan and former U.S. attorney general Janet Reno.

"What's next?" I asked Andrew, referring to my second ANTI- record.

"I have an idea."

"I'm not surprised."

"Ever hear of Drive-By Truckers?"

"Yes, but I haven't heard their music."

"Remember David Hood, the bass player in the Muscle Shoals Rhythm Section?"

"Yes."

"Well, his son Patterson and another musician, Mike Cooley, formed this southern-rock, country-flavored band called Drive-By Truckers."

When I listened to them, I didn't think they matched my style. But Andrew assured me that they would bend my way. I had doubts. I didn't think, for example, you could get the Basie band to play hip-hop.

Andrew made more arguments for the Truckers.

"They have an audience you need," he said. "Plus, they're a working band, and I love the idea of you going into a studio with a self-contained, hot-off-the-road working unit."

"That's because I'm a hot-off-the-road working singer."

"Exactly! It'll be a dream."

It was a nightmare, but the nightmare had a happy ending.

Patterson sent me sixty songs and I rejected all sixty. It felt more like six hundred. Andy sent me another batch. I didn't hear anything I liked. Kevin pitched in and found most of the ones I wound up singing. After weeks of deliberating, it came down to ten eclectic numbers, including Elton John's "Talking Old Soldiers," Don Henley's "You Don't Know Me at All," Willie Nelson's "Somebody Pick Up My Pieces," and "I Guess We Shouldn't Talk About That Now," cowritten by the brilliant Kim McLean.

At Kevin's suggestion, we recorded at FAME Studios in Muscle Shoals. I arrived with an expression on my face that Patterson Hood later described as "respect me or I'll whip your ass." The truth is, in the beginning of this project, I didn't feel respected. Drive-By Truckers had written no arrangements. Nothing had been planned. They wanted to wing it. I wanted to kill them. At this stage of my life, I'm an artist who wants to knock it out quickly. I don't have time to watch the musicians "find themselves" in the studio or in the song. When I saw the lack of preparation, I wanted to walk out. But Patterson proved to be as stubborn as I am.

For days we went to war in the studio. As they developed their approach to the music, I insisted that they heed my approach. The struggle wasn't easy. Finally, I threw a fit. I told them in no uncertain terms to stop doing it their way. "Goddamnit," I demanded, "just do it the way I'm singing it. Follow my body language." After my fit, the songs started coming together. It helped when Patterson brought in old-timers like his dad and keyboardist Spooner Oldham.

Patterson kept pushing me. He said, "I think we should write a song together."

"I don't write songs," I shot back. "I interpret them."

"But I've been taking notes of the things you've been saying since you got here, Bettye," Patterson explained, "and wrote a song."

He called it "The Ballad of Bettye LaVette." I rewrote it. Andrew got on piano and helped us find the right form. The song turned into "Before the Money Came." Kevin rewrote the subtitle: "The *Battle* of Bettye LaVette," a reflection of the creative fighting that characterized my work with the Truckers.

> *Close shooting don't kill no birds*
> *I'm standing tall with the rest of the girls*
> *Hanging on to my mama's every word*
> *Gonna sing them out loud and conquer the world*
> *All them faces on the pictures up there*
> *Make me remember when my table was bare*
> *Living at my mama's house*
> *Taking food from my family's mouth*
> *Before the money came*

I was singing R&B back in '62
Before you were born and your mama too
I knew David Ruffin when he was sober
Sleeping on my floor before he crossed over
All my friends on the Grammy shows
I was stuck in Detroit trying to open doors
Record deals kept falling apart
One with Atlantic nearly broke my heart
Before the money came

I got a lot to say
So proud I was built this way
Some folks didn't see my worth
Didn't know where I fit in
Forty years I kept on singing
Before the money started rolling in

There was a time when I would call it luck
If I got me a gig for fifty bucks
Now I've got all these big decisions to make
Never thought success would be hard to take
Shoes on my feet, more in the closet
Silk on my skin and more if I want it
All these years I've kept my style
I wouldn't cross over so it took me a while
Before the money came

Long time coming, it's just about time
I ain't never been afraid to speak my mind

I've always had a lot to say
So proud to be here, I'm gonna stay

I realize that I can be a stubborn bitch. I like things my way and I like things done promptly. *The Scene of the Crime* was not done promptly. The experience drove me up the wall. But in spite of my bellyaching, I have to admit it was worth the struggle. Drive-By Truckers really did have a sound. These songs required all the effort I had to give. When it was over, I was exhausted, pissed but pleased. ANTI- album number two was another worthy project that was well received. I had to admit that Andrew's idea was brilliant after all. He saw the title as an ironic reference to my initial recordings in Muscle Shoals. I didn't agree. But while I was doing *Crime*, I did notice the pictures of Aretha, Otis, Wilson Pickett, and many other superstars hanging on the walls of the studio. And I did tell owner Rick Hall, in no uncertain terms, that my picture needs to be up there as well.

For all the turmoil, I wound up loving the Truckers and the album we made together. I couldn't have been happier when it was nominated for a Grammy as Best Blues Album, even if it wasn't blues, and even if the artist who won wasn't a blues artist.

Muthafuckas.

There's a visual footnote to *The Scene of the Crime*, a poignant video where I sang Elton John and Bernie Taupin's "Talking Old Soldiers," a sad, sad song about days past and dreams lost. We shot it at the Locker Room Lounge in Detroit, one of my hangouts during my down days. Performing it, I sat at the bar, my head filled with memories. This was a bar where the big shots sat at one end and the no-counts sat at the other. I sat with the no-counts. I remember the stools reserved for the numbers girls. I remember the stool where Pervis Jackson of the Spinners sat. He'd have me climb on his lap, and he would give me a hundred-dollar bill so I could buy the family groceries. Pervis was one of the good guys. When he died, no one could sit on his stool in the Locker Room Lounge for a year. The old soldiers were gone, and it was a privilege to sing a song in their sweet memory.

My Nemesis,
My Gratitude

K evin had a brainstorm. Country singer George Jones was to be one of the recipients of the 2008 Kennedy Center Honors. I had done what many considered a killer version of his "Choices" on *The Scene of the Crime*. Maybe I could perform it at the Kennedy Center.

My agent at Rosebud wrote Michael Stevens, the show's producer, who looked me up on YouTube where he saw me singing "Little Sparrow." That was enough to convince him. But since everyone and his mother in Nashville wanted to sing a George Jones song, there was no place for me in that segment. On the other hand, how did I feel about singing a Who song?

I didn't know any. And when they sent me the one they wanted to do—"Love, Reign o'er Me"—it had nothing to do with my sensibility. It was wrong. But it was also a take-it-or-leave-it situation. If I wanted to sing in front of the president of the United

States on national television, it was either that or nothing. Well, I wasn't about to miss this chance. I had watched the Kennedy Center Honors for years. It was a show I had longed to be part of. Give me the goddamn song. I'll learn it. I'll sing it. I'll kill it.

I worked on a beautiful arrangement by Rob Mathes and located what I thought was the soul of the song. Naturally, I had to change some lyrics around because that was the only way it could work. This was a moment in the national spotlight, and I'd be goddamned if I wasn't going to make the most of it.

Slowly and proudly I walked to center stage at the Kennedy Center. I felt confident in a slim sleeveless maroon gown and matching maroon bejeweled earrings. I looked out in the audience. To my right was Aretha Franklin. To my left was Beyoncé. Up in the box, I saw Barbra Streisand, one of the honorees. With my well-honed sense of competition, I saw these women as my rivals. They were colleagues. Aretha and Barbra were my contemporaries. These were women I had wanted to engage with for years. I wanted to demonstrate to them that I was their equal, and then some. This was my chance to do just that.

I thought of Jim Lewis, who had said, "Learn to sing and you can sing anything anywhere." Well, that's what I was doing— singing an English rock song, in soul-ballad style, to an audience of dignitaries at one of the most prestigious venues in the country.

As I looked up, I saw tears on the face of Pete Townshend. I saw that Barbra was spellbound. Aretha did not let me out of her sight. Beyoncé held her breath.

When I sang the last line, the applause was thunderous.

At the post-concert reception, Roger Daltrey kneeled before me as though I were a queen, and sang my praises.

This, I thought, *is as close as I'll ever get to heaven.*

The video clip went viral on the Internet, and the next thing I knew, I was asked to sing a duet with Jon Bon Jovi on the steps of the Lincoln Memorial for President Obama's pre-inauguration concert aired on HBO around the world. This time they couldn't have picked a better song. Nothing could be more appropriate than Sam Cooke's "A Change Is Gonna Come." For many white people, the song was new. I had known it since the first week Sam sang it. For me, singing it was as easy as breathing. And yet singing in front of this international audience was the most overwhelming experience of my life . . . except when I had to learn to tap dance.

Change Is Gonna Come Sessions was the title of a download-only CD Andrew let me record for ANTI- in 2009. I was especially happy to have an opportunity to cut two challenging jazz standards—"Lush Life" and "'Round Midnight"—that had been haunting my heart and rattling around in my head for years. I sang it with the great Jim Lewis in mind, the man who described the accomplished vocalist as one for whom the boundaries of genre do not exist.

Genre jumping became my thing.

Because of the sensation caused by "Love, Reign o'er Me," Kevin and Andrew Kaulkin thought my third ANTI- album should be a collection of such songs. My husband suggested the title *Bettye's Banquet*. I had never heard of the Rolling Stones album that he was referencing, but I liked the way it sounded. My co-producer, Michael Stevens, wanted to call it *Interpretations: The British Rock Songbook*. Michael won. Since I really didn't know these songs, it would be another stretch. Stretching seems to be the theme of my old age.

At a time when many artists my age were singing the great American songbook, I asked myself some questions—*Why am I asked to stretch? Why do I have to fool with English rock tunes?* Well, why not? It worked with the Who and I figured it might with similar songs. Besides, I liked the irony that while Rod Stewart, the English rocker, was settling down with Gershwin, I, the American R&B singer, was tackling Pink Floyd.

There was an additional irony: These British hits dominated the airwaves at a time when I was struggling to keep my career going. The major soul singers like Gladys Knight and Aretha survived the British invasion, but many of us never found crossover success because America had gone crazy for the English. Now, in my golden years, here I was singing English rock. These songs, once my nemesis, might be my salvation.

After going over dozens of tunes, I realized there was a good reason I didn't know what they were about. When they wrote them, the rockers were stoned out of their minds. Acid scrambled many a British brain. So once again, I modified lyrics and sometimes rearranged the songs' structures so they made sense to me. In the case of Pink Floyd's "Wish You Were Here," I thought about my fallen friends like Marvin Gaye, David Ruffin, and Eddie Kendricks. With Paul McCartney's "Maybe I'm Amazed," I told the story of the difference my husband Kevin has made in my life. The Moody Blues' "Nights in White Satin" became a meditation on my relationship with my daughter. I was able to cast George Harrison's "Isn't It a Pity," Elton John's "Don't Let the Sun Go Down on Me," and Traffic's "No Time to Live" in a personal light. And in the end, strange as it seems, this album of British rock and roll—this collection of songs that a decade earlier I would have considered completely foreign to my identity— became highly autobiographical.

Fascinating, too, is the fact that my first appearance at the Hollywood Bowl came not during a rhythm-and-blues show but a Beatles tribute. The night was simultaneously serene and surreal. Stepping in front of a symphony orchestra and singing "Blackbird" to the lush accompaniment of a thousand and one strings brought tears to my eyes. That's when Eric Gardner, a major manager, heard me and asked to sign me. I was thrilled.

It was another instance of how hearing me on a record is one thing while hearing and seeing me live—as did Mike Kappus who led to Andrew Kaulkin who led to Eric Gardner—is another thing altogether. The big changes in my career have come as a result of my live performances. And my live performances came as the result of Jim Lewis's teachings.

There have also been moments of sweet revenge.

Janie Bradford, who cowrote "Money (That's What I Want)" with Berry Gordy, is one of my only female friends from the Motown era. (I must add Claudette Robinson, Smokey's first wife, to that list. Claudette is sweetness personified.) Janie was gracious enough to honor me at her yearly Heroes and Legends Banquet in Beverly Hills. All the old Motowners were in the grand ballroom, including the fattest cat of all, Berry Gordy. I walked out there proudly, aware that, of all the women my age, I was the only one who could still fit into an ultrasvelte size six gown. That made me feel great.

After accepting my statue onstage, I settled in at the podium. I spotted Mickey Stevenson in the audience. "You remember Mickey Stevenson," I said. "I've known him since he first began practicing being Berry Gordy." With one barb I paid him back for every disrespect and hurt he'd inflicted on me. "If I'm a hero at all," I continued, "it's because I have a daughter who's an inner-city school teacher in Detroit and two grandchildren in college. And if I'm a legend at all, it's because I know people in Detroit who Berry Gordy still owes fifty dollars to, from when they worked with him on the Chrysler line. I'd like to say that people in this room helped to get me where I am, but they didn't. But that's okay. I'm here, I'm standing tall, and I'm going to sing you a song."

A cappella, I sang "I Do Not Want What I Have Not Got" and got a standing ovation.

Afterward in the bar, G. C. Cameron, once a Spinner and then a Temptation, gave me news about Norman Whitfield, Motown's meanest producer.

"Norman's dead," said G.C.

I looked him in the eye and uttered a one-word reply. "Good."

G.C. nearly fell off the bar stool.

As I approach sixty-seven, I'm still not where I want to be, but I sure as hell ain't where I was.

I've had two years of extended engagements at Café Carlyle on Manhattan's Upper East Side. That's high cotton. It's where Bobby Short and Eartha Kitt once held court. It's one of the most prestigious cabaret gigs in the country, a warm intimate room that I love to play.

I also love Andrew Kaulkin and his record label of tattooed elves. He's stuck with me and helped me express my soul in interesting ways. He's the first music exec I've met who merits trust.

My circle of intimates isn't large, but it's precious. The lights of my life—my daughter, Terrye; my grandchildren, James and Marissa; my husband, Kevin; and my friends Robert Hodge, Jerome, David Freeland, and cousin Margaret—are the reasons that, at my advanced age, I'm still smiling every day.

I wish I were making more money and could travel in private jets like the British rockers whose songs I've sung, but I'm okay back there in coach. I'm still living for the city, but now there's more than one city. I'm playing London as well as Chicago, Sydney as well as Cincinnati.

I won't lie and tell you that it's easy. Before I hit the road, getting myself together to create a presentable Bettye LaVette takes all my effort. I'm a lot more relaxed staying home, tending to the backyard, the cats, and watching political news. My passion for old movies is stronger than ever. All I want to do is watch Bette Davis in *Now, Voyager* or Myrna Loy and William Powell in *The Thin Man*. The sublime glamour of those black-and-white masterpieces excites my imagination. Those are the images that coaxed me into show business in the first place. I love the depiction of a world inhabited by beautifully flawed people who drink martinis, decorate their homes with fabulous art deco furnishings, and speak with caustic wit. I envy their elegance and will not stop trying to emulate their sense of the sublime.

I also still love my champagne. There's a distinct possibility that, like my parents, I objectively can be called an alcoholic. If so, also like my parents, I am a highly functioning one. My drive to succeed has not been stymied by my fondness for intoxicants. And if my singing has improved over the years—and I do believe it has—my dependence on wine and marijuana has done nothing to impede that progress.

I'm going to smoke marijuana and drink until the doctors give me a death sentence. And even then, I may well continue smoking marijuana and drinking champagne.

A friend recently said that he read a book about how sex can get better in old age. I don't buy that. No one has enjoyed sex more than I have. It's one of the primary pleasures of my life, beginning when I was a teen. I'm so glad that I was free in an area where so many people are hung up. Along with cooking and singing, I've learned to fuck with the best of them. And yet, unlike singing and cooking, I can't say that sex is better than ever. It's still good, still important, and still a part of what I see as a healthy physical life. I have to say, though, that I don't have the energy I once did. Age will tire you out. The road will tire you out. And I don't care what you say, when you're in your sixties and fatigue is all over you, you just don't make love with the energy of crazed youth. Those days are gone.

I'm not about to give up my stubborn assertion that the church and its teachings can do more harm than good. If God wants to grab hold of me and convert me to his side, he knows where to find me. I'm not running from God, but neither am I chasing after him. I also do not view, as someone once suggested, music as my religion. Music's simply something I do, something I am, a restless force that, if it's not brought out, will drive me crazy. I have to do it. I don't know why, and at this point, I don't care why. I accept the fact that, the way some people are programmed to design buildings or knit sweaters or develop software, I'm programmed to sing.

Finally, my ability to get up to perform in public without making a fool of myself is due principally to Jim Lewis, my professor in all things musical. I still value the lessons learned from other men, not only remarkable musicians like Rudy Robinson, but lovers/friends like Ted White, Clarence Paul, Don Gardner, and Grover Washington, who, despite the complexities of our relationship, offered me genuine care. In my lifetime, I've learned a helluva lot more from pimps than preachers.

So to the people in the wild life and the respectable life, the people who have encouraged me and those who've blocked me, to the producers and the critics and the whores, the fans and the detractors and promoters, the supporters and the cynics, the gracious and the greedy, the honest and the crooked, the dealers and the dope fiends, to friends who are alive or dead, to everyone who has ever heard my voice and to those of you who have been patient enough to take the time to read my story, all I can say is . . . thank you. I like sharing this world with you. I like being alive.

Encore

While I was preparing my fourth record for ANTI-, which is to be released around the time of this book, I was sent a song from Kim McLean, a writer who really gets me. Before I go, I want to leave you with her words, which I recently recorded.

THE MORE I SEARCH (THE MORE I DIE)

I'm an open book, I ain't got no secrets
My story bleeds poetic lines
For all my deep introspection
It's still my heart that they can't find
They just go on, they just keep on talkin'
They never doubt the things they do
But as for me, I'm still a mystery
Eluded by the simple truth

In my vain humiliation
I've wandered through shame's dark halls
I've donned a new name, assumed me a new nature
Foolin' nobody, just creatin' walls
So many chances I've taken
So many choices I have made
I choose again, today, to seek love
God, if it's you, please let me in

The more I search, the more I die
I wanna feel, I wanna be alive
Am I saved, or am I broken?
Am I healed, or just justified?
The more I search, the more I die

Still I search to find me a vision
To feel ambition and dream once more
I've lost it all, but some folks say I'm lucky
Am I the victim, or did I just close the door?
So here I am, you can take me or leave me
But if you don't mind as you go
Give a little nod for mere compassion
For the sake of both our souls

The more I search, the more I die
I wanna feel, I wanna be alive
Am I saved, Lord, or am I broken?
Am I healed, or do ya think I'm just justified?
The more I search, the more I die
The more I search, the more I die

Acknowledgments

I would especially like to thank:

My mother, Pearl Haskins, who taught me so much more than I thought she did; my father, Frank Haskins, who adored me; my sister, Mattie, who taught me what it means to be a woman; Raymond Philpot, who taught me how to drive and brought me to Jim; Jim Lewis, who taught me what it means to be a singer; my daughter, Terrye; my grandchildren, Randall James and Marissa, whose future I look forward to; Margaret Nell Wilson, ofttimes my link to life; Robert Hodge, who is my never-failing hand; Jerome Andre ("Shavers"), so much a son to me, so sincere a friend; David Freeland, my intellectual muse, for whom I am so thankful; Dave Godin and Ralph McKnight, who unfortunately never got to see the results of their never-ending belief in me; Rudy Robinson, my music director for more than thirty years; John Goddard, the keeper of the crypt; Frederick Wilhelms III, to whom I will be forever grateful and will miss terribly; Mike Kappus, Tom Gold, and Rosebud (my booking agency), the first people to come to my aid. I thank them for their continued faith in me. Andrew Kaulkin and everyone at ANTI- (my record company), who have given me the complete freedom to sing anything that I wish. They have my undying gratitude. Tresa Redburn (my publicist) at Department 56, my red-lipped wonder; Eric Gardner (my manager) and Panacea Entertainment, who are helping me to write the next chapter; and Michael Stevens, who gave me my greatest shot. I will be forever grateful. David Ritz, for his patience and understanding and mad writing skills in helping to put this book together; my band (Alan Hill, Brett Lucas, Charles Bartels, and Darryl Pierce), who have been with me since this coming up out of the crypt. Last, but certainly not least, my husband, Kevin Kiley, who it took me fifty years to find and who I am sure I cannot live without.

The following are *all* people who have helped me in one way or another to get to this point: Willie Jones, Armicee Jones, Betty Chavis, Jerry Wexler, Don Gardner, Evans King, Mary Card, Donnie Sadler, Phil Parnell, Kimberly Ellis, Joycelyn Goins, Paul Williams, Gilles Pettard, David Cole, Dave Thomas, David Nathan, Andy and Allison Taylor, Bill and Stella Greensmith, Bryan James, Jon Tiven, Randall Grass, Dennis Walker, Rudy Calvo, Alan Mercer, Robert Mugge, Jay Sielman and the Blues Foundation, Norman Fidel, Richie and Vickie Noorigia, Bob Davis and the Soul Patrol, the Southern Soul Yahoo Group, the Soulful Detroit web forum, and David Rosenthal and Penguin Group (USA) for allowing me this new journey.

I would also like to thank Joe Rosen, Rene Hill, Julius "Juice" Freeman, Henry Moore, and David Hood for the photos.

Because I am so often asked who influenced me, and because I started singing at sixteen, I thought that *no one* had influenced me. However, giving it some thought, I have come up with the following. Here they are: R. H. Harris and his protégé Sam Cooke, Johnny Tanner of the Five Royales, Mahalia Jackson, Fred Astaire, Bing Crosby, Judy Garland, Roy Rogers, LaVerne Baker, Ruth Brown, Little Willie John, Hank Ballard, James Brown, Doris Day, Bobby Bland, Etta James, and Baby Washington.

And to all of the people who *could have* helped me when I needed help, and *didn't,* and the ones who hurt me and didn't have to (you only made me stronger) . . . well . . . you know who you are, and . . . well . . . *you* know . . .

David thanks the brilliant Bettye LaVette, one of my favorite artists and people in all the world; as well as Kevin Kiley, David Vigliano, Eric Gardner, Rabbi David Rosenthal, Vanessa Kehren, Aileen Boyle, Brian Ulicky, Gregg Kulick, Margaret Nell, and Robert Hodge. Love to my family—Roberta, Ali, Jess, Herny, Jim, Charlotte, Nino, James, Isaac, Elizabeth, Esther, beloved nieces and nephews, and especially Pops who, at ninety-five, inspires us all. Gratitude to Alan Eisenstock, Herb Powell, and Harry Weinger for undying support in times of need. I believe.

Selected Discography

Vinyl 45s/Singles

"My Man—He's a Lovin' Man" / "Shut Your Mouth"
    Atlantic 2160—1962 (No. 7 R&B, No. 101 Pop)

"You'll Never Change" / "Here I Am"
    Atlantic 2198—1963

"Witchcraft in the Air" / "You Killed the Love"
    LuPine 123—1963

"Let Me Down Easy" / "What I Don't Know (Won't Hurt Me)"
    Calla 102—1965 (No. 20 R&B, No. 103 Pop)

"I Feel Good (All Over)" / "Only Your Love Can Save Me"
    Calla 104—1965

"I'm Just a Fool for You" / "Stand Up Like a Man"
    Calla 106—1966

"I'm Holding On" / "Tears in Vain"
    Big Wheel 1969—1966

"Almost" / "Love Makes the World Go Round" (instrumental)
    Karen 1540—1968

"Get Away" / "What Condition My Condition Is In"
    Karen 1544—1968
"A Little Help from My Friends" / "Hey Love"
    Karen 1545—1969
"Let Me Down Easy" / "Ticket to the Moon"
    Karen 1548—1969
"He Made a Woman Outta Me" / "Nearer to You"
    Silver Fox 17—1969 (No. 25 R&B)
"Do Your Duty" / "Love's Made a Fool Out of Me"
    Silver Fox 21—1970 (No. 38 R&B)
"Games People Play" / "My Train's Comin' In"
    Silver Fox 24—1970
"Take Another Little Piece of My Heart" / "At the Mercy of a Man"
    SSS International 839—1970
"He Made a Woman Outta Me" / "My Train's Coming In"
    SSS International 933—1970
"Never My Love" / "Stormy"
    TCA 001—1971
"Heart of Gold" / "You'll Wake Up Wiser"
    Atco 6891—1972
"Your Turn to Cry" / "Soul Tambourine"
    Atco 6913—1973
"Thank You for Loving Me" / "You Made a Believer Out of Me"
    Epic 50143—1975 (No. 94 R&B)
"Behind Closed Doors" / "You're a Man of Words, I'm a Woman of Action"
    Epic 50177—1975
"Doin' the Best That I Can Pt. 1" / "Doin' the Best That I Can Pt. 2"
    West End 1213—1978
"Doin' the Best That I Can (Special New Mix)" / "Doin' the Best That I Can (Remix)"
    Mixes by Walter Gibbons, West End 22113-X—1978 (12-inch single)
"Right in the Middle (Of Falling in Love)" / "You Seen One You Seen 'Em All"
    Motown 1532—1982 (No. 35 R&B)

"I Can't Stop" / "Either Way We Lose"
    Motown 1614—1982
"Trance Dance Pt. 1" / "Trance Dance Pt. 2"
    Street King 1122—1984 (12-inch single)
"The Rhythm & the Blues" / "Have You Tried Jesus?" / "The Rhythm & the Blues"
    This 45 is from a musical that Bettye appeared in. Bettye is the featured vocalist on "Have You Tried Jesus?" Get Down 5484—1984
"Surrender" / "Time Won't Change This Love"
    Motorcity 39—1990 (12-inch single—UK)
"Good Luck" / "Good Luck" (instrumental)
    Motorcity 83—1991 (12-inch single—UK)
"Damn Your Eyes" / "Out Cold"
    Bar None—1997 (cassette-only single)
"Yours and Mine" / "Serendipity"
    The Dynamites, Outta Sight Records—2012
    Track: "Yours and Mine" (duet with Charles Walker)

CDs and LPs

Tell Me a Lie, Motown, 1982 (LP); Reel Music, 2008 (CD)
    Tracks: "Right in the Middle (Of Falling in Love)," "Either Way We Lose," "Suspicions," "You Seen One You Seen 'Em All," "I Heard It Through the Grapevine," "Tell Me a Lie," "I Like It Like That," "Before I Even Knew Your Name (I Needed You)," "I Can't Stop," "If I Were Your Woman"
Nearer to You: The SSS Recordings, Charly UK, 1990 (import CD); Snapper UK, 2012 (import CD)
    Tracks: "He Made a Woman Outta Me," "Nearer to You," "Do Your Duty," "Love's Made a Fool of Me," "My Train's Coming In," "Games People Play," "At the Mercy of a Man," "Piece of My Heart," "Let's Go, Let's Go, Let's Go" (with Hank Ballard), "Hello Sunshine" (with Hank Ballard), "We Got to Slip Around," "Easier to Say (Than Do)," "Let Me Down Easy" (Calla), "I'm in Love," "Feelings" (unreleased TCA), "Living Life on a Shoestring" (unreleased TCA)

Not Gonna Happen Twice, Motorcity, 1990 (import CD)
> **Tracks:** "Not Gonna Happen Twice," "Love Caught Me Out," "Out of the Blue," "Have a Heart," "Right Out of Time," "Too Great a Price to Pay," "Let Me Down Easy," "Good Luck," "Jimmy Mack," "Time Won't Change This Love," "Danger, Heartbreak Dead Ahead," "Surrender"

Living the Nightlife, Various Artists, Kent UK, 1993 (import CD)
> **Track:** "(Happiness Will Cost You) One Thin Dime" (recorded as a demo for Scepter Records in 1964)

Lost Soul, Various Artists, Sony, 1994 (CD)
> **Track:** "You're a Man of Words, I'm a Woman of Action"

The Very Best of the Motorcity Recordings, Motorcity, 1996 (CD)
> **Tracks:** "Good Luck," "Right Out of Time," "Have a Heart," "Jimmy Mack," "Let Me Down Easy," "Out of the Blue," "Time Won't Change This Love," "Not Gonna Happen Twice," "Surrender," "Too Great a Price to Pay," "I'm Ready for Love," "Love Caught Me Out," "Danger, Heartbreak Dead Ahead," "Reach for the Sky"

Betty LaVette & Carol Fran, Bluesoul Belles, The Complete Calla, Port & Roulette Recordings, West Side UK, 1999 (import CD); Emd Int'l, 2005 (import CD)
> **Tracks:** "Let Me Down Easy," "Only Your Love Can Save Me," "Stand Up Like a Man," "What I Don't Know "(Won't Hurt Me)," "Cry Me a River (Take 1)," "She Don't Love You Like I Love You (Take 5)," "I Feel Good All Over (Take 1)," "I'm Just a Fool for You (Take 2)"

Let Me Down Easy: In Concert, Munich, 2000 (import CD)
> **Tracks:** "My Man," "Damn Your Eyes," "Right in the Middle," "You'll Never Change," "Almost," "Your Turn to Cry," "He Made a Woman Outta Me," "Let Me Down Easy"

Souvenirs, Art & Soul, 2000 (import CD)
> **Tracks:** "It Ain't Easy," "Fortune Teller," "Our Own Love Song," "Soul Tambourine," "Your Turn to Cry," "Ain't Nothing Gonna Change Me," "All the Black and White Children," "If I Can't Be Your Woman," "Outside Woman," "The Stealer," "My Love Is Showing," "Souvenirs,"

"Heart of Gold," "You'll Wake Up Wiser," "My Man—He's a Lovin' Man," "Shut Your Mouth," "You'll Never Change," "Here I Am"

A Woman Like Me, Blues Express, 2003 (CD); W. C. Handy Award Winner for Best Comeback CD

Tracks: "Serves Him Right," "The Forecast," "Thru the Winter," "Right Next Door," "When the Blues Catch Up to You," "Thinkin' Bout You," "A Woman Like Me," "It Ain't Worth It After Awhile," "When a Woman's Had Enough," "Salt on My Wounds," "Close As I'll Get to Heaven," "Hey, Hey Baby (Bettye's Blues)"

Vanthology—A Tribute to Van Morrison, Various Artists, Evidence, 2003 (CD)

Track: "Real Real Gone"

Remembering Roots of Soul, Vol. 2: Birth of Motor Town, Various Artists, RPM/Shout UK, 2004 (import CD)

Tracks: "Witchcraft in the Air," "You Killed My Love"

I've Got My Own Hell to Raise, ANTI-, 2005 (CD); DBK Works, 2005 (LP)

Tracks: "I Do Not Want What I Have Not Got," "Joy," "Down to Zero," "The High Road," "On the Surface," "Just Say So," "Little Sparrow," "How Am I Different," "Only Time Will Tell," "Sleep to Dream"

Get In the Groove—Live, Various Artists, Norton, 2005 (CD)

Tracks: "Night Time Is the Right Time," "Tailfeather Finale"

Dirty Laundry: The Soul of Black Country, Various Artists, Trikont, 2005 (import CD); Trikont, 2009 (import vinyl)

Track: "What Condition My Condition Is In"

Take Another Little Piece of My Heart, Varèse Sarabande, 2006 (CD)

Tracks: "At the Mercy of a Man," "Do Your Duty," "Easier to Say (Than Do)," "Games People Play," "He Made a Woman Outta Me," "I'm in Love," "Hello Sunshine" (with Hank Ballard), "Love Made a Fool of Me," "My Train's Comin' In," "Nearer to You," "We Got to Slip Around," "Piece of My Heart," "Let's Go, Let's Go, Let's Go" (with Hank Ballard)

Child of the Seventies: The Complete Atlantic/Atco Recordings, Rhino Handmade, 2006 (CD)

Tracks: "It Ain't Easy" (LP version), "If I Can't Be Your Woman" (LP version), "Fortune Teller" (LP version), "Your Turn to Cry" (single version), "Soul Tambourine" (single version), "All the Black and White Children" (LP version), "Our Own Love Song" (LP version), "Ain't Nothing Gonna Change Me" (LP version), "Outside Woman" (LP version), "The Stealer" (LP version), "My Love Is Showing" (LP version), "Souvenirs" (LP version), "Waiting for Tomorrow" (previously unreleased), "Livin' Life on a Shoestring" (previously unreleased), "Your Turn to Cry" (mono single version), "Soul Tambourine" (mono single version), "Heart of Gold" (single version), "You'll Wake Up Wiser" (single version), "Here I Am" (single version), "You'll Never Change" (single version), "My Man—He's a Lovin' Man" (single version), "Shut Your Mouth" (single version)

Do Your Duty: The Complete Silver Fox Recordings, Sundazed, 2006 (LP); Sundazed, 2009 (CD)

Tracks: "My Train's Comin' In," "Do Your Duty," "Love Made a Fool of Me," "At the Mercy of a Man," "Piece of My Heart," "Easier to Say (Than Do)," "He Made a Woman Outta Me," "Nearer to You," "We Got to Slip Around," "I'm in Love," "Games People Play"

What's Going On, The Dirty Dozen Brass Band, Shout! Factory, 2006 (CD)

Track: "What's Happening Brother"

Song of America, Various Artists, Thirty Tigers, 2007 (CD)

Track: "Streets of Philadelphia"

The Scene of the Crime, ANTI-, 2007 (CD); ANTI-, 2007 (LP) Grammy Award Nomination for Best Contemporary Blues Album

Tracks: "I Still Want to Be Your Baby (Take Me Like I Am)," "Choices," "Jealousy," "You Don't Know Me at All," "Somebody Pick Up My Pieces," "They Call It Love," "Last Time," "Talking Old Soldiers," "Before the Money Came (The Battle of Bettye LaVette)," "I Guess We Shouldn't Talk About That Now"

The Lost Soul Gems, Various Artists, Sony Music Japan, 2008 (import CD)

Tracks: "You Made a Believer Out of Me," "You're a Man of Words, I'm a Woman of Action"

Change Is Gonna Come Sessions, ANTI-, 2009 (download-only EP)

Tracks: "Change Is Gonna Come," "'Round Midnight," "God Bless the Child," "Lush Life," "Ain't No Sunshine," "Ain't That Lovin' You Baby"

By the People, For the People: Music Inspired by the Motion Picture **By the People: The Election of Barack Obama,** Various Artists, Proceeds to United Way, 2010 (download from iTunes only)

Track: "A Change Is Gonna Come" (live duet with Jon Bon Jovi)

Live from the Artists Den: Season 2, Artists Den, 2010 (download from iTunes only)

Track: "Jealousy" (with Drive-By Truckers)

Interpretations: The British Rock Songbook, ANTI-, 2010 (CD; import LP); Grammy Award Nomination for Best Contemporary Blues Album

Tracks: "The Word," "No Time to Live," "Don't Let Me Be Misunderstood," "All My Love," "Isn't It a Pity," "Wish You Were Here," "It Don't Come Easy," "Maybe I'm Amazed," "Salt of the Earth," "Nights in White Satin," "Why Does Love Got to Be So Sad," "Don't Let the Sun Go Down on Me," "Love Reign o'er Me" (live)

Walter Gibbons—Jungle Music—Mixed with Love: Essential & Unreleased Remixes 1976-1986, Various Artists, Strut, 2010 (CD)

Track: "Doin' the Best That I Can" (Walter Gibbons 12-inch mix)

The 30th Annual John Lennon Tribute: Live from the Beacon Theatre NYC, Various Artists, Theatre Within, 2011 (download only)

Track: "The Word"

Dedicated: A Salute to the 5 Royales—Steve Cropper, 429 Records, 2011 (CD)

Tracks: "Don't Be Ashamed" (duet with Willie Jones), "Say It"

Chimes of Freedom: The Songs of Bob Dylan, Various Artists, Amnesty International, 2012 (CD), Honoring 50 Years of Amnesty International

Track: "Most of the Time"

Will Porter, Will Porter, 2012 (CD)

Track: "Make You Feel My Love" (duet with Will Porter)

Thankful N' Thoughtful, ANTI-, 2012 (CD) ANTI-, 2012 (LP)

Tracks: "Dirty Old Town," "Crazy," "Yesterday Is Here," "Thankful N' Thoughtful," "Time Will Do the Talking," "The More I Search (The More

I Die)," "I'm Not the One," "Everything Is Broken," "Fair Enough," "I'm Tired," "Everybody Knows This Is Nowhere," "Dirty Old Town" (alternate version)

Thankful N' Thoughtful, Deluxe Edition, ANTI-, 2012 (CD)

Tracks: "Dirty Old Town," "Crazy," "Yesterday Is Here," "Thankful N' Thoughtful," "Time Will Do the Talking," "The More I Search (The More I Die)," "I'm Not the One," "Everything Is Broken," "Fair Enough," "I'm Tired," "Everybody Knows This Is Nowhere," "Dirty Old Town" (alternate version), "Old" (bonus track), "Whole Lotta Lonely" (bonus track), "Welcome to the Good Times" (bonus track)

Unreleased tracks: "Baby Doll," (Big Wheel, 1966), "Light My Fire," (Karen, 1968), "Close to You" (TCA, 1971), "Stormy" (alternate version; TCA, 1971), "Raindrops Keep Fallin' on My Head" (TCA, 1971), "No Way to End a Love Affair" (TCA, 1978), "Dancing in the Streets" (TCA, 1978), "Bend a Little" (TCA, 1978), "Tell Me a Lie" (original; 1978), "Losing Your Love" (1978), "Brickyard Blues" (2006), "Instant Karma" (ANTI-, 2009), "Save Some Time to Dream" (ANTI-, 2012)

WANTED

I am searching for audio copies of any of my Schaefer Beer or Salem Cigarette commercials. For that and any other inquiries, please contact my management company, Panacea Entertainment, at: info@panacea-ent.com.

Index

Index